`No More Curried Eggs For Me`

`No More Curried Eggs For Me`

A concoction of classic comedy sketches
compiled by ROGER WILMUT

METHUEN·LONDON

First published in Great Britain in 1982 by
Methuen London Ltd,
11 New Fetter Lane, London EC4P 4EE
Reprinted 1982
First published in this Methuen Paperback edition
in 1983
Printed in Great Britain
by Richard Clay (The Chaucer Press) Ltd
Bungay, Suffolk

ISBN 0 413 53680 7

CONTENTS

6   *Contents*

PREFACE

It's going to be a bit complicated to explain this book. . . . Several years ago I wrote a book called *The Goon Show Companion*, which had a number of script extracts. Then I wrote *Tony Hancock: 'Artiste'*, which had quite a few script extracts. Then I wrote *From Fringe to Flying Circus*, which had a lot of script extracts.

So my publishers said, 'Why don't you just put a lot of script extracts together and never mind about the boring bits in between?' . . . nice people, I get on well with them . . . so anyway, I did, and this is it.

The idea is, they are supposed to be everybody's favourite funny sketches from radio and television – or anyway, some of them. They are mostly transcribed from the original broadcasts rather than copied from the actual scripts, in order to reflect the last-minute changes which are almost always made to performances (what writers call 'mucking up a perfectly good script').

Incidentally, I didn't invent the title . . . I just couldn't think of a better one. It is supposed to encapsulate the whole idea of funny scripts as reflected in its psychological representation of the spirit of comedy, or something like that. You'll find it, in its original context, in one of the sketches in this book.

My thanks are due to the people who actually *wrote* all this stuff, and who very kindly allowed me to use it; and to Helen Carrasso, Peter Copeland, Anne Dent, Nick Hern, Neil Koenig, Vaughan Lipscombe, Tim Smith and D. Jeremy Stevenson for the loan of records and tapes or help in the selection of items.

ROGER WILMUT

`AT LAST THE 1948 SHOW`

This predecessor to *Monty Python's Flying Circus* consisted of two series of programmes broadcast by Independent Television in 1967. The sketch included here was written by John Cleese and Graham Chapman, and was first broadcast on 1 March 1967; the performers were Cleese himself and Marty Feldman, then at the beginning of his career as a television and film performer.

`Bookshop`

CLEESE: Good morning, sir.

FELDMAN: Good morning, can you help me? Do you have a copy of *Thirty Days in the Samarkand Desert with a Spoon* by A.J. Elliott?

CLEESE: No, we haven't got it in stock, sir.

FELDMAN: How about *A Hundred-and-One Ways to Start a Monsoon*?

CLEESE: By . . .?

FELDMAN: An Indian gentleman whose name eludes me for the moment.

CLEESE: Well, I don't know the book, sir.

FELDMAN: Not to worry, not to worry. Can you help me with *David Copperfield*?

CLEESE: Ah, yes, Dickens.

FELDMAN: No.

CLEESE: I beg your pardon?

FELDMAN: No, Edmund Wells.

CLEESE: I think you'll find Charles Dickens wrote *David Copperfield*.

FELDMAN: No, Charles Dickens wrote *David Copperfield* with two 'p's – this is *David Coperfield* with *one* 'p' by Edmund Wells.

CLEESE: Well in that case we don't have it.

FELDMAN: Um – funny, you've got a lot of books here.

CLEESE: Yes, we do have quite a lot of books here, but we don't have *David Coperfield* with one 'p' by Edmund Wells. We only have *David Copperfield* with two 'p's by Charles Dickens.

FELDMAN: Pity – it's more thorough than the Dickens.

CLEESE: More *thorough*?

FELDMAN: Yes – I wonder if it's worth having a look through all the *David Copperfields* . . .

CLEESE: No, no, I'm quite sure that all our *David Copperfields* have two 'p's.

FELDMAN: Probably, but the original by Edmund Wells also had two 'p's – it was after that that they ran into copyright difficulties.

CLEESE: No, I'm quite sure that all our *David Copperfields* with two 'p's are by Charles Dickens.

FELDMAN: How about *Great Expectations*?

CLEESE: Ah yes, we have that . . .

FELDMAN: That's *G-r-a-t-e Expectations*. Also by Edmund Wells.

CLEESE: Well in that case we don't have it – we don't have anything by Edmund Wells, actually – he's not very popular.

FELDMAN: Not *Nicholas Nickleby*? That's *K-n-i-c-k-e-r*, *Knickerless*?

CLEESE: No.

FELDMAN: Or *Christmas Carol* with a 'q'?

CLEESE: No, definitely not.

FELDMAN: Sorry to trouble you.

CLEESE: Not at all.

FELDMAN: I wonder if you have a copy of *Rarnaby Budge*?

CLEESE: No, as I say, we're right out of Edmund Wells.

FELDMAN: No, not Edmund Wells – Charles Dickens.

CLEESE: Charles Dickens?

FELDMAN: Yes.

CLEESE: You mean *Barnaby Rudge*.

FELDMAN: No, *Rarnaby Budge* by Charles Dickens – that's Dikkens with two 'k's, the well-known Dutch author.

CLEESE: No, no – we don't have *Rarnaby Budge* by Charles Dikkens with two 'k's the well-known Dutch author, and perhaps to save time I should add right away that we don't have *Carnaby Fudge* by Darles Tikkens, nor *Stickwick Stapers* by Miles Pikkens with four 'm's and a silent 'q', why don't you try the chemist?

FELDMAN: I have – they sent me here.

CLEESE: Did they.

FELDMAN: I wonder if you have *The Amazing Adventures of Captain Gladys Stoat-pamphlet and Her Intrepid Spaniel Stig among the Giant Pygmies of Corsica*, Volume Two?

CLEESE: No, no, we don't have that one – funny, we've got quite a lot of books here.

FELDMAN: Yes, haven't you.

CLEESE: Well, I mustn't keep you standing around all day . . .

FELDMAN: I wonder . . .

CLEESE: No, no, we haven't. – I'm closing for lunch now . . .

FELDMAN: But I thought I saw it over there.

CLEESE: Where?

FELDMAN: Over there.

CLEESE: What?

FELDMAN: Olsen's *Standard Book of British Birds*.

CLEESE: Olsen's *Standard Book of British Birds*?

FELDMAN: Yes.

CLEESE: O-l-s-e-n?

FELDMAN: Yes.

CLEESE: B-i-r-d-s?

FELDMAN: Yes.

CLEESE: Yes, well we do have that one.

FELDMAN: The expurgated version, of course.

CLEESE: I'm sorry, I didn't quite catch that.

FELDMAN: The expurgated version.

CLEESE: The *expurgated* version of Olsen's *Standard Book of British Birds*?

FELDMAN: Yes. It's that one without the gannet.

CLEESE: The one without the gannet? They've all got the gannet – it's a standard bird, the gannet – it's in all the books.

FELDMAN: Well I don't like them, long nasty beaks they've got.

CLEESE: Well you can't expect them to produce a special edition for gannet-haters!

FELDMAN: Well, I'm sorry, I specially want the one without the gannet.

CLEESE: All right! *(Tears out the illustration.)* Anything else?

FELDMAN: Well, I'm not too keen on robins.

CLEESE: Right! Robins – robins . . . *(Tears them out.)* No gannets, no robins – there's your book!

FELDMAN: I can't buy that – it's torn!

CLEESE: It's torn! So it is! *(Throws it away.)*

FELDMAN: I wonder if you've got . . .

CLEESE: Go on, ask me another – we've got lots of books here – this is a bookshop, you know!

FELDMAN: How about *Biggles Combs His Hair*?

CLEESE: No, no, no, we don't have that one, no, no, funny – try me again.

FELDMAN: Have you got *Ethel the Aardvark Goes Quantity Surveying*?

CLEESE: No, no, we haven't got – which one?

FELDMAN: *Ethel the Aardvark Goes Quantity Surveying.*

CLEESE: *Ethel the Aardvark*? I've seen it! We've got it! Here! Here! Here! *Ethel the Aardvark Goes Quantity Surveying.* There! Now – *buy it*!

FELDMAN: I haven't got enough money on me.

CLEESE: I'll take a deposit!

FELDMAN: I haven't got *any* money on me.

CLEESE: I'll take a cheque!

FELDMAN: I haven't got a cheque-book.

CLEESE: It's all right, I've got a blank one!

FELDMAN: I don't have a bank account.

CLEESE: Right! I'll buy it for you! *(Rings it up.)* There we are, there's your change – that's for the taxi on the way home—

FELDMAN: Wait, wait, wait . . .

CLEESE: WHAT? WHAT?

FELDMAN: I can't read!

CLEESE: Right – *SIT!* . . . 'Ethel the Aardvark was trotting down the lane one lovely summer day, trottety-trottety-trot, when she saw a Quantity Surveyor. . . . . .'

ROWAN ATKINSON (RICHARD SPARKS

The youngest performer represented here, Rowan Atkinson, in his first four years of showbusiness starred in his own single half hour show *Canned Laughter*, the award-winning *Not the Nine O'Clock News* and his own one-man show which played a sell-out three-month season in the West End and for which he won the SWET award for comedy performance of the year. He also appeared in two charity shows for Amnesty International; *The Secret Policeman's Ball* and *The Secret Policeman's Other Ball* in 1981. This monologue written by Richard Sparks is taken from the 1979 Amnesty Show.

Rowan read Electrical Engineering at Newcastle University and Engineering Science at Oxford and it was whilst at Oxford that he was widely noticed in the 1977 Oxford Revue.

`Schoolmaster`

Right, quiet . . . Ainsley . . . Babcock . . . Bland . . . Carthorse . . . Dint . . . Ellsworth-Beast Major . . . Ellsworth-Beast Minor . . . Fiat . . . German . . . Haemoglobin . . . Havvernut . . . Jones M. . . . Jones N. . . . Kosygin . . . Loudhailer . . . Muttock . . . Nancy-Boy Potter . . . Nibble . . . (Come on, settle down) . . . Orifice . . . Plectrum . . . Poins . . . Sediment . . . Soda . . . Ta . . . Ta? . . . Undermanager . . . Wickett . . . Williams Wickett . . . Williams Wycherley . . . Wycherley Wickett . . . Wycherley Williams . . . and Wycherley Williams Wockett . . . Zob . . . absent.

All right, your essays. 'Discuss the contention that Cleopatra had the body of a roll-top desk and the mind of a duck'. Oxford and Cambridge Board 'O' Level paper 1976. Don't fidget, Bland. The answer – 'yes'. Jones M., Orifice, Sediment and Undermanager – see me afterwards. Most of you of course didn't write nearly enough – Dint, your answer was unreadable – put it *away*, Plectrum. If I see it once more this period, Plectrum, I shall have to tweak you. Do you have a solicitor? You're lying, Plectrum, so I shall tweak you anyway. See me afterwards to be tweaked – yes, *isn't* life tragic. Don't sulk, boy, for God's sake – has Matron *seen* those boils? (Horrid little twerp.)

Bland, German, Nancy-Boy Potter, Undermanager – cribbing. Undermanager, answer upside-down. Do you do it deliberately, Undermanager? You're a moron, Undermanager, what are you? A carbuncle on the backside of humanity.

Don't snigger, Babcock – it's not funny. *Antony and Cleopatra* is not a funny play. If Shakespeare had meant it to be funny he would have put a joke in it. There is no joke in *Antony and Cleopatra* – you'd know that if you'd read it, wouldn't you, Babcock? Pest.

What play of Shakespeare's *does* have a joke in it then? Anyone? . . . *The Comedy of Errors*, for God's sake. *The Comedy of Errors* has the joke of two people looking like each other. Twice. It's not that funny, German.

And the other Shakespearean joke is . . . Nibble? . . . NIBBLE! *LEAVE ORIFICE ALONE*! What a lot!

Right, for the rest of this period you will write about Enobarbus. Undermanager – just try and write 'Enobarbus'. Either way up, boy, I'm not bothered. Usual conditions – no referring, no eating, no cheating, no looking out of the windows, no slang, no slide rules. Use ink only – via a nib if possible. You may use dividers, but not on each other.

Kosygin – you're in charge.

ALAN BENNETT

One of the four performers made famous by *Beyond the Fringe*, Alan Bennett has in more recent years moved into the field of television and theatrical play writing. This monologue – a late addition to *Beyond the Fringe*, also included in his television series *On the Margin* – is quoted here in the version he performed at the 1976 Amnesty Gala Performance *A Poke in the Eye with a Sharp Stick*, an occasion on which he displayed his disconcerting ability to look twenty years younger, and sound twenty years older, than his real age.

'Telegram'

Hello? . . . Hello – hello – I want to send a telegram, please, if I may. Yes – well, I am the subscriber, and my name is Desmond. Yours is Glynis? Yes, my *surname* is Desmond . . . Yours is Budd . . . We seem to be drifting into a relationship of somewhat redundant intimacy . . . My address – one hundred and sixty, Victoria Terrace, N.W.1, telephone number 246-8045. And the telegram is going to a Miss Tessa Prosser, that's Tessa Prosser, 130 Chalcott Square, S.W.19.

Right. Right. Er – no, 'Right, right' is *not* the telegram – what I will do, I will say 'Here is the telegram', and then anything I say subsequent to that will be the telegram.

Here is the telegram. . . . . . Are you still there? No, no, no . . . that's not it, no – the telegram is: 'Bless – your – little' . . . 'Bless your little' . . . 'Bottibooes' . . . *'Bottibooes'* . . . I've never been called upon to spell it, I suppose it's B-O-double-T-I-B-double-O-E-S – though I think probably the last E is not statutory. Well, it's a diminutive of 'bottom', I suppose . . . No, Miss Prosser *doesn't* have a diminutive bottom – that's partly the joke, you see . . . anyway . . . and I want to sign it, um – 'Desmond Donkey-drawers'. Well, it's a term of affection Miss Prosser is wont to use at moments of heightened excitement.

Well, that's the whole of the message, then I want to round it off by the word 'Norwich'. Norwich. Well, it's an idiomatic way of saying, 'Knickers Off Ready When I Come Home'. You see, it's the initial letters of each word. Yes. I *know* 'knickers' is spelt with a 'k', I was at Oxford, it was one of the first things they taught us. And in a perfect world I suppose it would be 'Korwich' – but I don't think that carries quite the same idiomatic force.

'Burma' – no, I hadn't come across that one – what's that?

'Be Upstairs Ready My Angel'. Yes, well I like that, it's very nice – ah – I don't think it would be appropriate in this case for strictly topographical reasons – because Miss Prosser in fact lives in a basement flat. And if she were 'upstairs ready', she would in fact be in the flat of the window-dresser from Bourne and Hollingsworth – and I don't think she would want that. And I certainly don't think he would.

That's it then . . . what? Obscene? 'Norwich'? Oh, I certainly don't think so, no, I mean – what about the Bishop of Norwich? When he signs his letters 'Cyril Norwich', does he *mean* 'Cyril Norwich', or 'Cyril Knickers-off-ready-when-I-come-home'? No . . . goodbye, goodbye.

PETER COOK

Peter Cook's straight-faced character E.L. Wisty first came to prominence when Cook performed a number of monologues on ITV's 1965 series *On the Braden Beat*; but the original character goes back to 1960 and *Beyond the Fringe*, although at that stage he had no name. Since the monologue was semi-improvised and changed from night to night, there is no 'authentic' text: here is the published version. On the gramophone records it is known as 'Sitting on a Bench' — here I have called it simply

'Miner'

Yes, I could have been a judge but I never had the Latin, never had the Latin for the judging, I just never had sufficient of it to get through the rigorous judging exams. They're noted for their rigour. People come staggering out saying, 'My God, what a rigorous exam—' And so I became a miner instead. A coal miner. I managed to get through the mining exams – they're not very rigorous, they only ask you one question, they say 'Who are you?' and I got seventy-five per cent on that—

Of course, it's quite interesting work, getting hold of lumps of coal all day, it's quite interesting. Because the coal was made in a very unusual way. You see, God blew all the trees down. He didn't just say let's have some coal. As He could have done, He had all the right contacts. No, He got this great wind going, you see, and blew down all the trees, then, over a period of three million years, He changed it into coal, gradually over a period of three million years so it wasn't noticeable to the average passer-by. It was all part of the scheme, but people at the time did not see it that way. People under the trees did not say, 'Hurrah – coal in three million years', no, they said, 'Oh dear, oh dear, trees falling on us – that's the last thing we want', and of course their wish was granted.

I am very interested in the universe – I am specializing in the universe and all that surrounds it. I am studying Nesbitt's book – *The Universe and All That Surrounds It, An Introduction*. He tackles the subject boldly, goes from the beginning of time right through to the present day, which according to Nesbitt is 31 October 1940. And he says the earth is spinning into the sun and we will all be burnt to death. But he ends the book on a note of hope, he says, 'I hope this will not happen'. But there's not a lot of interest in this down the mine.

The trouble with it is the people. I am not saying you get a load of riffraff down the mine, I am not saying that, I am just saying we had a load of riffraff down my mine. Very boring conversationalists, extremely boring, all they talk about is what goes on in the mine. Extremely boring. If you were searching for a word to describe the conversations that go on down the mine, boring would spring to your lips. – Oh God! They're very boring. If ever you want to hear things like: 'Hello, I've found a bit of coal. Have you really? Yes, no doubt about it, this black substance is coal all right. Jolly good, the very thing we're looking for.' It is not enough to keep the mind alive, is it?

Whoops. Did you notice I suddenly went *whoops*? It's an impediment I got from being down the mine. 'Cause one day I was walking along in the dark when I came across the body of a dead pit pony. Whoops, I went in surprise, and ever since then I've been going *whoops* and that's another reason I couldn't be a judge, because I might have been up there all regal, sentencing away, 'I sentence you to whoops', and you see, the trouble is under English law that would have to stand. So all in all I'd rather have been a judge than a miner.

And what is more, being a miner, as soon as you are too old and tired and sick and stupid to do the job properly, you have to go. Well, the very opposite applies with the judges. So all in all I would rather have been a judge than a miner—

Because I've always been after the trappings of great luxury you see, I really, really have. But all I've got hold of are the trappings of great poverty. I've got hold of the wrong load of trappings, and a rotten load of trapping they are too, ones I could've very well done without.

DUD AND PETE

Strangely, Peter Cook and Dudley Moore hardly worked together in sketches when they were in *Beyond the Fringe*, and it was not until their television series *Not Only . . . But Also* that they created the classic couple Dud and Pete – the idiot who knows nothing and the idiot who knows everything. This early sketch comes from the second programme in the first series, broadcast on BBC-2 on 23 January 1965.

'Sex Fantasies'

DUD: All right, then, Pete, are you?

PETE: Not too bad, you know, not too bad . . . Cheers.

DUD: What you been doing lately, then?

PETE: Well quiet, pretty quiet, not been up to much – I had a spot of the usual trouble the other day.

DUD: Oh, did you – what happened, then?

PETE: A spot of the usual trouble – well, I come home about half-past eleven – we'd been having a couple of drinks, remember? – I come home about half-past eleven, and, you know, I was feeling a bit tired, so, you know, I thought I'd go to bed, you know, take me clothes off, and so on, you know.

DUD: 'Sright – well, don't you take your clothes off *before* you go to bed?

PETE: Er – no, I made that mistake this time, got it the wrong way round – anyway, I got into bed, settled down, I was just about, you know, reading *The Swiss Family Robinson*.

DUD: Good, ain't it.

PETE: It's a lovely book, Dud, a lovely book – an I got up to about page 483 second paragraph, when suddenly – 'bring, bring – bring, bring'.

DUD: What's that?

PETE: That's the 'phone, going 'bring, bring'. So I picked up the 'phone, and – you know who it was?

DUD: Who?

PETE: Bloody Betty Grable. Calling transatlantic, bloody Betty Grable – I said, 'look, Betty, what do you think you're doing, calling me up half-past eleven at night?' She said 'It's half-past two in the afternoon over here'. I said, 'I don't care what bloody time it is, there's no need to wake *me* up'. She said, 'Peter, Peter – get on a plane, come dance with me, be mine tonight'.

DUD: I thought it was the middle of the afternoon?

PETE: Yes, what she probably meant was 'be mine tonight tomorrow afternoon our time'.

DUD: No – didn't she mean tomorrow afternoon – er—

PETE: Anyway, 'Be mine tonight', she said – I said, 'Look, Betty – we've had our laughs, we've had our fun, but it's all over'. I said, 'Stop pestering me, get back to Harry James and his trumpet – stop pestering *me*' I said, I slammed the 'phone down and said 'Stop pestering me'.

DUD: Shouldn't you have said 'Stop pestering me' *before* you slammed the 'phone down?

PETE: I should have, yes . . .

DUD: It's funny you should say that, 'cos a couple of nights ago, you remember, we had a couple of drinks—

PETE: I remember that, yes . . .

DUD: —and I came home, you know, I was going to bed, felt a bit tired – I was having a nightcap—

PETE: 'Course you were—

DUD: —and I was just dropping off nicely, and all of a sudden I heard this hollering in the kitchen.

PETE: Hollerin'?

DUD: And screaming and banging on the door, you know, and I thought I must have left the gas on – so, I go down there – I fling open the door – you never guess – it's bloody Anna Magnani, up to her knees in rice, screaming at me – 'Lesse more entrate – amore me por favore!'

PETE: Italian.

DUD: Italian, yes – she was covered in mud, she grabbed hold of me, she pulled me all over the floor – she had one of them see-through blouses—

PETE: All damp, showing everything through it—

DUD: Yes, and we rolled all over the floor – I hit her, I said

'Get out of here! Get out of here, you Italian . . . thing!' I said. 'Get out of here', I said . . .

PETE: 'You Italian thing . . .' a good thing to call her.

DUD: Yes – I said, 'Don't you come here and mess up *my* rice again, mate'.

PETE: I should hope not. I had the same bloody trouble about three nights ago – I come in, about half-past eleven at night, we'd been having a couple of drinks I remember – and I come in, I get into bed, you see, feeling quite sleepy. I could feel the lids of me eyes beginning to droop – a bit of the droop in the eyes – I was just about to drop off, when suddenly 'tap, tap, tap' at the bloody window pane – I looked out – you know who it was?

DUD: Who?

PETE: Bloody Greta Garbo! Bloody Greta Garbo – stark naked save for a shortie nightie. She was hanging on to the window sill, and I could see her knuckles all white . . . saying 'Pieter, Pieter, ...' – you know how these bloody Swedes go on – I said, 'Get out of it!' – bloody Greta Garbo. She wouldn't go – she wouldn't go, I had to smash her down with a broomstick, poke her off the window sill, she fell down on the pavement with a great crash . . .

DUD: She just had a nightie on, is that all?

PETE: That's all she had on, Dud, just a—

DUD: See-through?

PETE: —a see-through, shortie nightie. Nothing else – except for her dark glasses, of course. Dreadful business.

DUD: Well, it's funny you should say that—

PETE: Yes, it's funny I should say that.

DUD: —four nights ago, I come home, we'd been having a couple of drinks—

PETE: Couple of drinks, yes . . .

DUD: —I come home, I come through the door, and – sniff –
sniff, sniff, I went – you know – funny smell, I thought,
smells like wood burning—

PETE: Probably burning wood, Dud.

DUD: What's that?

PETE: 'Burning Wood' – that's a perfume worn by sensual,
earthy women.

DUD: Funny you should say that, because I come in the
bathroom, you know, I thought, 'bit stronger here', you
know, 'sfunny – I come in the bedroom, – it's getting
ridiculous, this smell, you know, so I get into bed, you
know, turn the covers back – it's a bit warm in bed – I
thought 'funny', you know, being warm like that – and –
I get into bed, I put out the light – and, I was just going off
to kip – and suddenly, I feel a hand on my cheek.

PETE: Which cheek was that, Dud?. . . . Come on – which
cheek was it?

DUD: It was the left upper. I said, I thought, you know,
'funny' . . . I turned on the light – bloody hand here,
scarlet fingernails—

PETE: Who was it?

DUD: You never guess – bloody Jane Russell.

PETE: Jane Russell?

DUD: Jane Russell, in bed with me, stark naked – I said,
'Jane' . . .

PETE: With the huge . . .

DUD: With the things . . . I said, 'Jane', I said, 'get out of
here' . . .

PETE: Get out . . .

DUD: 'Get out of here', I said, 'you may be mean, moody and
magnificent, but as far as I'm concerned it's all over'. So I

threw her down – I took her out of bed, threw her down the stairs – I threw her bra and her – er – gauze panties after her, I threw them down . . . and the green silk scarf . . . I said, 'Get out of here! Get out of here, you hussy!' . . . I threw her fag holder – I threw it down the stairs after her – I threw a bucket of water over her, I said, 'Get out of here, you hussy!' – I said, 'don't come in my bed again, mate, it's disgusting!' Terrible – I was shocked to the quick.

PETE: You're quite right, you got to do something about these bloody women who pester you . . .

DUD: What you doing tonight, then?

PETE: Well, I thought we might go to the pictures.

`FAWLTY TOWERS`

Fawlty Towers has proved to be one of the most popular of all television comedy series, despite there having been only twelve programmes. Written by John Cleese with his then wife Connie Booth, it provided him with his classic characterization as Basil Fawlty, owner of the worst hotel in Torquay. Probably the favourite of all the shows is the last of the first series, broadcast on BBC-2 on 24 October 1975; the final section is quoted here. Basil has been knocked unconscious during a fire at the hotel; suffering from the after-effects of concussion he escapes from the hospital and comes back to the hotel, where a party of German guests is expected.

BASIL FAWLTY	John Cleese
MANUEL	Andrew Sachs
POLLY	Connie Booth
DOCTOR	Louis Mahoney
GERMANS	Nick Kane
	Willy Bowman
	Dan Gillian
	Lisa Bergmayr

`The Germans`

BASIL *(masterfully)*: Manuel!

MISS TIBBS: Oh, Mr Fawlty!

BASIL: Ah, good evening.

MISS TIBBS: Are you all right now?

BASIL: Perfectly, thank you. *(To Manuel.)* Take this to the room please, dear.

(Manuel takes the case, somewhat taken aback.)

MISS GATSBY: Are you sure you're all right?

BASIL: Perfectly, thank you. Right as rain.

(He makes his way a little unsteadily towards the desk, but misses. He re-appears and goes correctly to his position behind the desk. Manuel rushes up.)

MANUEL: You OK?

BASIL: Fine, thank you dear. You go and have a lie-down.

MANUEL: Que?

BASIL: Ah, there you are. Would you take my case . . . how did you get that?

MANUEL: What?

BASIL: Oh never mind . . . take it . . . take it upstairs!

MANUEL: Que?

BASIL: Take it . . . take it . . .

MANUEL *(staring)*: I go get Polly.

BASIL: I've already had one. Take it!

MANUEL: What?

BASIL: Take it, take it now . . . *(Manuel hurries off.)* Tch! The people I have to deal with . . .

(He looks up to see a couple approaching the desk. he beams at them.)

ELDERLY GERMAN: Sprechen Sie Deutsch?

BASIL: . . . Beg your pardon?

E. GERMAN: Entschuldigen Sie, bitte, können Sie Deutsch sprechen?

BASIL: . . . I'm sorry, could you say that again?

GERMAN LADY: You speak German?

BASIL: Oh, German! I'm sorry, I thought there was something wrong with you. Of course, the Germans!

GERMAN LADY: You speak German?

BASIL: Well . . . er . . . a little . . . I get by.

GERMAN LADY: Ein bisschen.

E. GERMAN: Ah – wir wollen ein Auto mieten.

BASIL *(nodding helpfully)*: Well, why not?

E. GERMAN: Bitte.

BASIL: Yes, a little bit tricky . . . Would you mind saying it again?

GERMAN LADY: Please?

BASIL: Could you repeat . . . amplify . . . you know, reiterate? Come on! Yes?

E. GERMAN: *Wir* . . .

BASIL: Wir? . . . Yes, well we'll come back to that.

E. GERMAN: . . . Wollen . . .

BASIL *(to himself)*: Vollen . . . Voluntary?

E. GERMAN: Ein Auto mieten.

BASIL: Owtoe . . . out to . . . Oh, I see! You're volunteering to go out to get some meat. Not necessary! *We have meat here*!

(Pause; the couple are puzzled.)

BASIL *(shouting very loudly)*: Vee haf meat hier . . . in ze buildink!

(He mimes a cow's horns.)

BASIL: Moo.

(Polly comes in.)

BASIL: Ah, Polly, just explaining about the meat.

POLLY: Oh! We weren't expecting you.

BASIL: Oh, weren't you? *(Hissing through his teeth.)* They're

Germans. Don't mention the war . . .

POLLY: I see. Well Mrs Fawlty said you were going to have a rest for a couple of days, you know, in the hospital.

BASIL *(firmly)*: Idle hands get in the way of the devil's work, Fawlty. Now . . .

POLLY: Right, well, why don't you have a lie-down, and I can deal with this.

BASIL: Yes, yes, good idea, good idea Elsie. Yes. Bit of a headache, actually . . .

MISS TIBBS: We don't think you're well, Mr Fawlty.

BASIL: Well perhaps not, but I'll live longer than you.

MISS GATSBY: You must have hurt yourself.

BASIL: My dear woman, a blow on the head like that . . . is worth two in the bush.

MISS TIBBS: Oh, we know . . . but it was a nasty knock.

BASIL: Mmmmmmmm . . . Would you like one?

(He hits the reception bell impressively.)

BASIL: Next please.

(At this moment four more guests come down the stairs.)

BASIL *(a hoarse whisper)*: Polly! Polly! Are these Germans too?

POLLY: Oh yes, but I can deal . . .

BASIL *(urgent and conspiratorial)*: Right, right. Here's the plan. I'll stand there and ask them if they want something to drink before the war . . . before their lunch . . . *don't mention the war*!

(He moves in front of the guests, bows, and mimes eating and drinking.)

1ST GERMAN: Can we help you?

(Basil gives a startled jump.)

BASIL: Ah . . . you speak English.

1ST GERMAN: Of course.

BASIL: Ah, wonderful! Wunderbar! Ah – please allow me to

introduce myself – I am the owner of Fawlty Towers, and
may I welcome your war, your wall, you wall, *you all* . . .
and hope that your stay will be a happy one. Now would
you like to eat first, or would you like a drink before the
war . . . ning that, er, trespassers will be – er, er, – tied up
with piano wire . . . Sorry! Sorry! *(Clutches his thigh.)* Bit
of trouble with the old leg . . . got a touch of shrapnel in
the war . . . *Korean*, Korean War, sorry, Korean.

1ST GERMAN: Thank you, we will eat now.

*(Basil bows graciously and ushers the party into the dining
room.)*

BASIL: Oh good, please do allow me. May I say how pleased
we are to have some Europeans here now that we are on
the Continent . . .

(They all go in. Polly meanwhile is on the phone.)

POLLY: Can I speak to Doctor Fin please?

(Cut to dining room; Basil is taking the orders.)

BASIL: I didn't vote for it myself, quite honestly, but now
that we're in I'm determined to make it work, so I'd like to
welcome you all to Britain. The plaice is grilled, but that
doesn't matter, there's life in the old thing yet . . . No,
wait a moment, I got a bit confused there. Oh yes, the
plaice is grilled . . . in fact the whole room's a bit warm,
isn't it . . . I'll open a window, have a look . . . And the
veal chop is done with rosemary . . . that's funny, I
thought she'd gone to Canada . . . and is delicious and
nutritious . . . in fact it's *veally* good . . . *veally* good?

1ST GERMAN: The veal is good?

BASIL: Yes, doesn't matter, doesn't matter, never mind.

2ND GERMAN: May we have two eggs mayonnaise please?

BASIL: Certainly, why not, why not indeed? We are all
friends now, eh?

1ST GERMAN *(heavily)*: A prawn cocktail . . .

BASIL: . . . All in the Market together, old differences forgotten, and no need at all to mention the war . . . Sorry! . . . Sorry, what was that again?

1ST GERMAN: A prawn cocktail.

BASIL: Oh prawn, that was it. When you said *prawn* I thought you said war. Oh, the war! Oh yes – completely slipped my mind, yes, I'd forgotten all about it. Hitler, Himmler, and all that lot, I'd completely forgotten it, just like that. *(He snaps his fingers.)* . . . Sorry, what was it again?

1ST GERMAN *(with some menace)*: A prawn cocktail . . .

BASIL: Oh yes, Eva Prawn . . . and Goebbels too, he's another one I can hardly remember at all.

2ND GERMAN: And ein *pickled herring*!

BASIL: Hermann Goering, yes, yes . . . and von Ribbentrop, that was another one.

1ST GERMAN: And four cold meat salads please.

BASIL: Certainly, well I'll just get your hors d'oeuvres . . . hors d'oeuvres vich must be obeyed at all times without question . . . Sorry! Sorry!

POLLY: Mr Fawlty, will you call your wife immediately?

BASIL: Sybil!! . . . Sybil!! . . . she's in the hospital you silly girl!

POLLY: Yes, call her there!

BASIL: I can't, I've got too much to do. Listen . . . *(He whispers through his teeth.)* Don't mention the war . . . *I* mentioned it once, but I think I got away with it all right . . . *(He returns to his guests.)* So it's all forgotten now and let's hear no more about it. So . . . that's two egg mayonnaise, a prawn Goebbels, a Hermann Goering and four Colditz salads . . . no, wait a moment, I got a bit confused there, sorry . . .

(One of the German ladies has begun to sob.)

BASIL: I got a bit confused because everyone keeps mentioning the war, so could you please . . .

(The 1st German, who is comforting the lady, looks up angrily.)

BASIL: What's the matter?

1ST GERMAN: It's all right.

BASIL: Is there something wrong?

1ST GERMAN: Will you please stop talking about the war?

BASIL: Me? You started it!

1ST GERMAN: We did not start it.

BASIL: Yes you did, you invaded Poland . . . Here, this'll cheer you up, you'll like this one, there's this woman, she's completely stupid, she can never remember anything, and her husband's in a bomber over Berlin . . .

(The lady howls.)

BASIL: Sorry! Sorry! Here, here, she'll love this one . . .

1ST GERMAN: Will you leave her alone?

BASIL: No, this is a scream, I've never seen anyone not laugh at this!

1ST GERMAN *(shouts)*: Go away!

BASIL: Look, she'll love it – she's German!

(Places a finger under his nose preparatory to doing his Hitler impression.)

POLLY: No, Mr Fawlty!! . . . do Jimmy Cagney instead!

BASIL: What?

POLLY: *Jimmy Cagney*!

BASIL: Jimmy Cagney?

POLLY: You know . . . 'You dirty rat . . .'

BASIL: I can't do Jimmy Cagney!

POLLY: Please try . . . 'I'm going to get you . . .'

BASIL: Shut up! Here, watch – who's this, then?
  (He places his finger across his upper lip and does his Führer party piece. His audience is stunned.)
BASIL: I'll do the funny walk . . .
  (He performs an exaggerated goose-step out into the hall, does an about-turn, and marches back into the dining room. Both German women are by now in tears, and both men on their feet.)
BOTH GERMANS: *Stop it*!!
BASIL: I'm trying to cheer her up, you stupid Kraut!
1ST GERMAN: It's not funny for her.
BASIL: *Not funny*? You're joking!
1ST GERMAN: Not funny for her, not for us, not for any German people.
BASIL *(amazed)*: You have absolutely no sense of humour, do you!
2ND GERMAN *(shouting)*: *This is not funny*!
BASIL: *Who won the bloody war, anyway*?
  (The doctor comes in, with a hypodermic needle ready.)
DOCTOR: Mr Fawlty, you'll be all right – come with me.
BASIL: Fine.
  (Suddenly Basil dashes off through the kitchen, out across into the lobby and into the office. He spots the medical men in pursuit and leaves by the other door into reception. He meets Manuel under the moose's head, and thumps him firmly on the head; Manuel sinks to his knees. The moose's head falls off the wall; Basil is knocked cold. The moose's head lands on Manuel. The Major, entering from the bar, is intrigued.)
MANUEL *(speaking through the moose's head)*: Oooooh, he hit me on the head . . .
THE MAJOR *(slapping the moose's nose)*: No, you hit *him* on the head. You *naughty* moose.
1ST GERMAN *(sadly)*: However did they win?

`THE FROST REPORT`

David Frost first rose to fame in BBC Television's satirical series *That Was The Week That Was*. When the satire boom began to die, he transferred neatly to less polemical comedy in his series *The Frost Report*, which in effect presented a string of gags and sketches on a different subject each week. John Cleese and the 'Two Ronnies' – Barker and Corbett – were teamed in a series of short sketches in which the three of them stood in a line facing the camera and gave different viewpoints on different subjects. In this sketch, written by Marty Feldman and John Law, the subject is given additional point by their heights – Cleese's six foot five inches, Barker's five foot eight-and-a-half inches, and Corbett's five foot one inch. It was broadcast on BBC-1 on 7 April 1966.

`Three Men on Class`

CLEESE: I look down on him *(indicating Barker)* because I am upper-class.

BARKER: I look up to him *(indicating Cleese)* because he is upper-class; but I look down on him *(indicating Corbett)* because he is lower-class. I am middle-class.

CORBETT: I know my place. I look up to them both. But I don't look up to him *(Barker)* as much as I look up to him *(Cleese)*, because he has got innate breeding.

CLEESE: I have got innate breeding, but I have not got any money. So sometimes I look up *(bending knees and doing so)* to him *(Barker)*.

BARKER: I still look up to him *(Cleese)* because although I have money, I am vulgar. But I am not as vulgar as him *(Corbett)*, so I still look down on him *(Corbett)*.

CORBETT: I know my place. I look up to them both; but while I am poor, I am honest, industrious and trustworthy. Had I the inclination, I could look down on them. But I don't.

BARKER: We all know our place, but what do we get out of it?

CLEESE: I get a feeling of superiority over them.

BARKER: I get a feeling of inferiority from him *(Cleese)*, but a feeling of superiority over him *(Corbett)*.

CORBETT: I get a pain in the back of my neck.

`THE GOON SHOW`

Of all the comedy programmes from radio's heyday in the 1950s, the *Goon Show* is remembered with most affection. More than any other show it broke down the barriers of radio – and indeed of comedy itself – and its inspired craziness has had a lasting effect on the British sense of humour. One of the best scripts, 'Dishonoured', was originally broadcast on 14 December 1954; when, during a later series, producer John Browell needed a script because Spike Milligan had been unable to provide one, he resurrected 'Dishonoured'. With only minor variations from the original it proved one of the best of all the *Goon Shows*, and was included on the first LP record of the Goons.

NEDDIE SEAGOON .... Harry Secombe
ECCLES
MORIARTY .... Spike Milligan
MINNIE BANNISTER
'MATE' (WILLIAM)
HERCULES GRYTPYPE-THYNNE
HENRY CRUN .... Peter Sellers
MAJOR DENNIS BLOODNOK
BLUEBOTTLE
ANNOUNCER .... Wallace Greenslade

Script by Spike Milligan

First broadcast 26 January 1959 in the BBC Home Service

`Dishonoured-Again`

GREENSLADE: This is the BBC Home Service. From the book, *I Knew Terence Nuke* by Eileen Beardsmore-Lewisham, tiddley-do spot, we present the play *I Knew Terence Nuke* from the *book* by Eileen Beardsmore-Lewisham.

ORCHESTRA: FORSYTE SAGA TYPE MUSIC.

GRAMS: DISTANT MOURNFUL HOOT OF FOG HORNS ON RIVER.

PETER: It can be cold in London, dam' cold. On such a night as this eighty years ago, a ragged idiot staggered into a forty-year-old fog-laden Limehouse area . . .

GRAMS: SLOW APPROACH OF PAIR OF BOOTS ALONG COBBLED HOLLOW-SOUNDING STREET. APPROACH-ING. STOP.

SEAGOON: It's me, folks, Neddy Seagoon. Here it is Christmas Eve and still no offers of pantomime, and not a penny have I towards a plate of vittles for me poor half-starved eighteen-stone body, so I'll lay me poor old twenty-stone head down on this eight-stone Embankment bench. Ahhh – this is nice and soft.

ECCLES: Dat's 'cause you're layin' on me.

SEAGOON: Hullo, hullo!

ECCLES: Hullo, hullo! . . . I wouldn't mind, but I got friends to tea.

MATE: Here, you two men, what you doing there? Come on, move along, that bench is for Royalty of no fixed abode.

SEAGOON: Constable have pity – 'tis Christmas, the time of good will.

MATE: 'Strewth, so it is! Well well, a merry Christmas on yer, mate.

SEAGOON: Same to you.

MATE: Now move along 'fore I belt yer.

MORIARTY: A moment, Law Guardian . . . Tiff Tuff Tang.

SEAGOON: The voice came from a man with a military bearing which he tossed in the air and caught. He emerged from the darkness and walked into the light.

FX: HITTING A LAMP POST.

MORIARTY: Oww! . . . Now, policeman, how would you like to join the river police?

MATE: I'd like that, sir.

MORIARTY: Huh!

GRAMS: ONE SPLASH.

MATE *(off)*: Thank you sir. A merry Christmas to you, sir.

MORIARTY: And a merry Christmas to you.

SEAGOON: The stranger now turned his glance on me. He observed my shredded paper suit, my thrice turned overcoat, my toes sticking out at the end of my feet.

MORIARTY: Down on your luck?

SEAGOON: Why are you interested in me?

MORIARTY: I run a rag and bone shop.

SEAGOON: Looking for a manager?

MORIARTY: No, I'm looking for stock. However, I have a friend of mine, a Bank Manager in the Bank of Twickenham, the Honourable Thynne, Grytpype-Thynne . . . how are you at mathematics?

SEAGOON: I speak it fluently.

MORIARTY: Touché.

SEAGOON: Three-ché.

MORIARTY: Very well, take this tray and present yourself to him tomorrow.

ORCHESTRA: LIGHT CHORDS.

GREENSLADE: Seagoon's wife was overjoyed at Ned's luck. He started work as a bank clerk with every prospect of becoming one.

SEAGOON: My wages were eight shillings a week, with an

allowance of three shillings for each child.

THYNNE: This brought his money up to eighty pounds a week.

SEAGOON: That was the manager, Mr Thynne, well-known in concentric circles.

THYNNE: Mr Seagoon – how long have you been with us?

SEAGOON: Twenty minutes.

THYNNE: What a splendid record of devotion and honesty. Neddie – (and this is where the story really starts) – Neddie, I'm putting you in a position of trust – you're going to be in charge of the gold vault. Here's the key.

SEAGOON: Gold? *Goldddd* – ha ha ha goldd – lovely gold – I'll be rich – no more rags for me – Golddd *(goes off)* Golddd . . .

THYNNE: I wonder if he's the right man for the job?

SEAGOON: I decided to pinch the gold. Immediately I backed a large horse-drawn motor van up to the front entrance of the bank.

MATE: You can't park that there, sir.

MORIARTY: Constable, how would you like to join the river police?

MATE: I'd like that very much, sir.

GRAMS: SPLASH.

MATE *(off)*: Thank you very much, sir.

MORIARTY: And a merry Christmas. Now carry on Neddie.

THYNNE: Yes – it's a lovely day for carrying on Neddie.

SEAGOON: Right. Next I carefully disguised myself as a Zulu warrior of the Matabele rising. So cunning was my make-up, not even my own grandmother would have recognized me.

SPIKE *(throat – old girl)*: Hello Neddie.

SEAGOON: Hello Grannie. In this inconspicuous disguise I

took the gold from the vaults and loaded it on to the van –
for three hours I toiled back and forth.

THYNNE: Oh, Neddie?

SEAGOON *(aside)*: Curses! I'm spotted.

THYNNE: Why are you wearing that leopard skin?

SEAGOON: So *that's* why I'm spotted!

THYNNE: Tell me, where are you taking that gold?

SEAGOON *(aside)*: I had to think of a good excuse.

THYNNE: You're stealing it, aren't you, Neddie.

SEAGOON: Blast – why didn't I think of that?

THYNNE: We'll have to give you a week's notice.

SEAGOON: Why? What have I done?

THYNNE: Nothing – but we're having to cut down on staff –
you see, there's been a robbery. You get that van started
while I get my hat and coat.

SEAGOON: You coming too?

THYNNE: There's no point in staying – there's more money in
the van than there is in the bank.

SEAGOON: Very well – we'll be partners.

THYNNE: Shake.

SEAGOON: I gave him my hand.

THYNNE: I gave him my foot – it was a fair swop.

SEAGOON: Ying tong iddle I po.

THYNNE: Good. For no reason – Max Conks Geldray.

SEAGOON: Huzzah!

*GELDRAY AND ORCHESTRA: 'IT'S ONLY A PAPER
MOON'.*

(Applause.)

GREENSLADE: 'Dishonoured – Part Two' – (And this is where
the story really starts). With their new-found wealth, Ned
painted the town red. Then the first blow fell.

FX: DOOR OPENS.

THYNNE: Neddie – bad news – the bank you stole the gold from – told the police!

SEAGOON: What a rotten trick – is nothing sacred?

THYNNE: Give yourself up, Neddie.

SEAGOON: Give myself up? No – I can't break myself of that habit. What about the gold?

THYNNE: Leave that with Moriarty – and when you come out in eighty-nine years – we will be waiting for you, won't we Moriarty?

SEAGOON: No, no – I couldn't keep you waiting all that time.

THYNNE: Then you'll have to go abroad – won't he, Moriarty?

SEAGOON: Abroad. But my wife – I can't leave her with thirty-eight children!

THYNNE: Isn't that enough?

SEAGOON: Yes – I suppose the rest would do her good.

THYNNE: And it would do you good too – you naughty boy.

SEAGOON: Mmm – how will I get the gold out of the country?

THYNNE: Oh, you box clever there – you leave the gold with us, and when you return – we'll be waiting.

SEAGOON: I'll flee the country – we sail at dawn – tonight!!!!!!

ORCHESTRA: SEA THEME.

SEAGOON: Within a week we were on board a private yacht, sailing West Nor-East South. I stood on the pilchard with the spanker blowing through my hair and the salty bloaters spinning before the goblets – it's a man's life, I tell 'ee – ha ha ha – a man's life, I tell 'ee . . .

GRAMS: JELLY SPLOSH.

THYNNE: I'm so sorry, Ned – never throw into the wind.

SEAGOON: Hello Captain Thynne – what's our position?

THYNNE: Desperate – I mean I'll enquire . . . Navigator? Can you restitute our position in the Med.?

ECCLES: Hel-ooooo dere . . .

THYNNE: What's that object off the port beam?

ECCLES: Yer — what *is* that object off the port beam?

SEAGOON: Good heavens — it's the Albert Hall!

ECCLES: Ooooooooh. You been to sea before.

THYNNE: But what is the Albert Hall doing off Beachy head?

SEAGOON: More to the point — what is this ship doing in Hyde Park?

ECCLES: Well the sea's calmer here.

THYNNE: You idiot — we're four thousand miles off course.

ECCLES: Well, nobody's perfect.

THYNNE: Shut up, Eccles.

MATE: I'm sorry, you can't park this yacht here.

MORIARTY: Constable, how would you like to join the Kensington Round Pond Police?

MATE: There ain't no such force.

GRAMS: SPLASH.

MORIARTY: You're the first!

MATE *(off)*: Thank you, sir.

ORCHESTRA: VICTORY AT SEA THEME.

GREENSLADE: 'Dishonoured — Part Three': In the Mediterranean (and this is where the story really starts). In the Med. the blow fell. One morning Neddie was called to the Kipten's Cabon.

THYNNE: Neddie — Neddie, when you came aboard I believe you deposited all the gold in the care of Moriarty.

SEAGOON: Yes — why, isn't it safe with him?

THYNNE: It's perfectly safe — wherever he and his rowing boat are.

SEAGOON: The gold I stole — stolen? The thief — which way did he go?

THYNNE: I pointed a finger.

SEAGOON: Ahhh! . . .

GRAMS: BOOTS RUN ALONG DECK AND DIVE OVERBOARD. ... SPLASH.

MORIARTY: Has he gone?

THYNNE: Yes – now let's go down and divide the gold, Moriarty.

(Goes off laughing.)

ORCHESTRA: TATTY LINK – A TERRIBLE MESS – BAND NOISES EVERYWHERE – CHISHOLM SINGS A BIT, ETC. ETC.

GRAMS: SPLASHING IN THE SEA.

SEAGOON: Meantime, I foundered alone in the Indian Ocean, unable to speak a word of the language. I swam on my back, side, front and knees, but I just couldn't get off to sleep.

MATE: I must ask you to move along there, sir.

SEAGOON: Ohh – it's you, constable – I thought you were in the river police?

MATE: That's right, sir.

SEAGOON: Then what are you doing in the Ocean?

MATE: I been promoted, sir.

SEAGOON: Congratulations – could you direct me to India?

MATE: Just follow the tramlines.

SEAGOON: Thank you. And so saying I struck out for the shore.

GREENSLADE: Ten miles he swam – the last three were agony.

SEAGOON: They were over land. Finally I fell in a heap on the ground. I've no idea who left it there. Then I heard the approach of a high-powered horseless carriage with a long dongler attachment and a brown card with the word 'Fertangg' on it in Greek.

GRAMS: OLD CROCK – BACK-FIRES – KLAXON HORN –

GRINDING GEARS.

CRUN: Hold tight Min – we're doing three miles an hour.

MIN: We'll all be murdered in our beds! Oh dear . . .

CRUN: Put the brake on, Minnie.

MIN: It doesn't suit me, Henry . . . Where is it, Hen?

CRUN: In a brown paper parcel under my seat.

MIN: Stand up, then.

CRUN: I can't stand up, Motoring Min – I'll lose my leather control . . .

GRAMS: CAR BREAKS DOWN – A GUSH OF STEAM.

CRUN: Oh dear, Min – the wick in the engine's gone out.

SEAGOON: *(Groans.)*

MIN: What's that? Oh – it's a young man . . . what are you doing under our car?

SEAGOON: I'm not doing anything under your car.

MIN: Thank heaven for that.

CRUN: I am Henry Motoring Crun – we are anxious to know if you need succour.

SEAGOON: Yes, just what I need – a glass of succour.

CRUN: Why don't you answer us, sir?

MIN: Hit him on the conk, Henry.

SEAGOON: Are you both deaf? I've told you I'm weak from exhaustion. *(Pause.)* Of course, that's why they can't hear me – I'm unconscious!

MIN: Come on, Henry – you heard what he said – he's unconscious.

CRUN: Help me lift him up Min – I'll take his head, and you – no, no – you go round the other side of his head.

MIN: Other side? . . . Oh dear . . .

FX: PAIR OF BOOTS WALKING ON GRAVEL GOING AWAY.

MIN *(long walk – off)*: O.K. – lift, Henry.

BOTH *(struggle)*: Ohhh – mnk – ahhhhhh.

GREENSLADE: Now, here is 'Dishonoured – Part Four'. Tied to the back of Crun's car, Seagoon was towed back to Poona – but the rope broke and left him stranded in the Indian Quarter of Bombay.

ORCHESTRA: WOG MUSIC.

SEAGOON: Yes – in the street of a thousand households – there is a place where a man can drink and forget his sorrows.

FX: TAP ON DOOR. DOOR OPENS.

PETER *(Indian)*: What does the dirt-encrusted sahib desire – all the sensuous drinks of the orient are yours – the pan beedy – the scented visnu wine – the Toddy juice – the aromatic crab pani – which do you desire, oh wicked one?

SEAGOON: Pot of tea, please.

SPIKE *(Indian)*: Ladies and European-type Gentlemen – take your European-type partners for the English-style cabaret.

RAY ELLINGTON QUARTET: 'FROM THIS MOMENT ON'.

(Applause.)

SPIKE: Everyone back to your own beds please. Now for the second part of the cabaret the mysterious Burra Bibby – oriental Queen will do the 'Dance of the Seven Army Surplus Blankets'.

POGGY*: SOLO OBOE VERY SOFTLY – WOG STYLE.

SEAGOON: Into the middle of the floor sprang a creature who sent my pulses racing. One by one the blankets fell to the floor – the lights went down, and as the last blanket fell

---

*Band member and master saxophonist, E.O. Pogson.

from the passionate creature I moved to her side in the dark. *(Panting.)* Oh desirable creature – what prompts you to dance in this den of vice?

ECCLES: I got to make a livin' too, you know.

SEAGOON: Eccles? You're not a woman!

ECCLES: *I* know that – but don't tell the manager.

SEAGOON: Why not?

ECCLES: We're engaged. It's going to be hell, folks.

SEAGOON: How did you get here?

ECCLES: Well, that fellow Moriarty and Grytpype-Thynne – they threw me into the sea.

SEAGOON: So there is some good in them.

ECCLES: Der question is – what are we gonna do now?

SEAGOON: I'm going to clear my name and get back my self-respect – I'll – I'll join the Navy!

ORCHESTRA: NAVAL POT-POURRI.

SEAGOON: No – I'll join the Army. It's too darn noisy in the navy. Come, Eccles . . .

ORCHESTRA: BLOODNOK LINK.

GRAMS: ALAMEIN BARRAGE – CHICKENS CLUCKING.

BLOODNOK: Bleiough . . . Aeioughhhhhhhhhh Bleioughhhhhh, oh – no more curried eggs for me. So you two naughty men want to join the Bombay Irish, do you?

SEAGOON: Aye aye, Jock mon.

BLOODNOK: Well, it's a tough life, I'll tell you – do you know what it's like to be in the thick of a bloody battle with bullets flying and sabres clashing?

SEAGOON: No.

BLOODNOK: Pity – I was hoping you'd tell me what it was like – you see I'm writing a book entitled *Bloodnok V.C.* However, let us take the Regimental Oath. Ready? Open your wallets and say after me – Help Yourself.

ECCLES AND SEAGOON: Help yourself.

BLOODNOK: Thank you. Next — do you swear to be brave soldiers?

BOTH: Yes.

BLOODNOK: Never turn a back on the enemy.

BOTH: Never.

BLOODNOK: Always speak well of a lady.

BOTH: Always.

BLOODNOK: And respect the chastity of a woman.

BOTH: Yes.

BLOODNOK *(angry)*: Have we got nothing in common? Still, we are in need of a couple of ripe steamers, you see the Red Bladder is raising the Pathan Tribes — he's got fresh consignments of automatic swords and a touch of the Rangoon Krut thrown in.

SEAGOON: Where's he get the finance?

BLOODNOK: Two international crooks smuggled him a shipload of gold saxophones.

SEAGOON *(to himself)*: Grytpype and Moriarty? So *that's* the game. *(Aloud.)* Sir — I have a score to settle — let *me* go to the frontier.

BLOODNOK: Right, sign this.

SEAGOON: Neddie — Seagoon. There, am I a soldier now?

BLOODNOK: I've no idea, I only collect autographs.

FX: DOOR BURSTS OPEN.

ELLINGTON: Major Bloodnok sir, and this is where the story really starts —

BLOODNOK: What is it, Muriel?

ELLINGTON: The Red Bladder is lighting fires all along the fireplaces.

BLOODNOK: What? Seagoon — arm the men to the teeth.

SEAGOON: Impossible.

BLOODNOK: No arms?

SEAGOON: No teeth.

BLOODNOK: Then we can't fight.

SEAGOON: Sir, I want a chance to prove I'm a man.

BLOODNOK: Report to the M.O.

SEAGOON: I'll fight the mad Mullah — clear me name — recover the gold — and capture Moriarty and Grytpype-Thynne into the bargain — who will ride with me?

BLUEBOTTLE: Ensign Bluebottle will! *(Applause.)* Thank you, thank thank you . . . see, my sword is in my hand.

FX: CLANG.

BLUEBOTTLE: Ooh, the end's fallen off.

SEAGOON: Little Jug-Head Bugler blow the alarm.

BLUEBOTTLE: That is what I say — blow the alarm — can we play another game, please?

SEAGOON: This is no game, little drooping seat . . . Get mounted, lad.

BLUEBOTTLE: Yes my capatain, I am mounteded and ready for the ride — I say, wait a minute — what's this in the saddlebag?

SEAGOON: That's dynamite, lad.

BLUEBOTTLE: Here — you're not starting that lark again?

SEAGOON: We'll soon know the valid truth. To horse!

ECCLES: Can I come too?

BLUEBOTTLE: It's about time you came to, heu heuh . . . I made a little jokule!

ECCLES: I'll get him . . . here — guess what I'm getting for my birthday?

BLUEBOTTLE: What are you getting, Eccules?

ECCLES: I'm getting a bow-wow.

BLUEBOTTLE: Ohh! I'm not getting a bown-wown . . . I'm getting a junior smoker's kit, complete with toffee ashtray and liquorice dog-ends.

ECCLES: I like liquorice. My mother says that liquorice gives you a good run for your money.

SEAGOON: To the Khyber Pass. . . . . . Fooooooooooorward!

GRAMS: HORSES' HOOVES GALLOPING OFF WITH STIRRING BUGLE CALL (FAMOUS DUBBING).

SEAGOON: All that night I rode, and through the best part of the next day.

BLUEBOTTLE: You left the worst part to us – he he – a joke by me.

FX: SLAPSTICK.

BLUEBOTTLE: Oh – my prules are funed!

SEAGOON: Haaalt – and this is where the story really starts.

GRAMS: HOOVES STOP.

BLUEBOTTLE: Oooooooeigh look my capatain, look – points cardboard finger at thousands of savage naughty men with indian bare bumpy old chests.

SEAGOON: The Red Bladder and his fifty thousand balloons – Gad – we're outnumbered twenty to one!

ECCLES: Twenty to one – time for lunch.

SEAGOON: We've only one chance – Bluebottle – ride to the crest of that crag and signal Major Bloodnok.

BLUEBOTTLE: What is the message?

SEAGOON: Tell him to keep two late dinners.

BLUEBOTTLE: I will do it – I will – ride, Vaquero, ride . . . here, wait a minute – Captain – in between me and that crag is a dirty big wide chasm, with a forty thousand foot drop to the raging torrent below.

SEAGOON: Fear not, shivering nut. That Arab stallion will bound that chasm like – like a wingèd arrow.

BLUEBOTTLE: Yes it will . . . get up, Dobbin.

FX: HORSE STARTS OF – GATHERS PACE – THEN

SUDDEN SILENCE.

(*Pause.*)

GRAMS: HEAVY SPLASH.

BLUEBOTTLE: Eheu! You rotten swine horse you – you did not jump over that chasm, and I have been hurled into the dreaded canyon – splat thud zowie blun thud – and several other rock hitting nut sounds.

MORIARTY: Welcome to the Indian River Police, little boy of mine.

BLUEBOTTLE: Oh, you are the forces of evils Morraynati man – thinks – I know how to get rid of the dynamite . . . Mr Moranatu – would you like a nice big long red cigar with a wick on the end?

FX: MATCH.

GRAMS: CRACKLING OF FUSE.

MORIARTY: Ohh, thank you little boy.

GRAMS: WHOOSH.

BLUEBOTTLE (*miles off*): is it nice?

MORIARTY: It's gone out.

GRAMS: APPROACH WHOOSH.

BLUEBOTTLE (*gasping*): I'll light it again for you . . .

GRAMS: MASSIVE EXPLOSION.

GRAMS: THE HARRY LIME THEME.

SPIKE: Thought you'd like to hear it again.

GREENSLADE: 'Dishonoured – part the last' – Neddie Seagoon gives his all in battle with the Red Bladder.

GRAMS: WOG BATTLE SCENE. HORSES GALLOPING. BUGLE CALLS. SALVO OF CANNONS. WOGS JUMPING UP AND SHOUTING.

BLOODNOK: How that battle raged – I heard it on the wireless, you know. Seagoon fought like a madman – how else? But alas – (*sobs*).

GRAMS: DISTANT MUTED BUGLE.

GREENSLADE: On that spot is now a little white stone.

CRUN: Yes – once a year Min lays flowers on it.

MIN: The stone bears a simple inscription in Hindustani.

BLOODNOK: I haven't the heart to tell her that, roughly translated, it says 'Bombay forty-nine miles'. Goodnight.

ORCHESTRA: OLD COMRADES MARCH.

GELDRAY AND ORCHESTRA: PLAY OUT – CRAZY RHYTHM.

TONY HANCOCK

Arguably the greatest British comedian since the second world war, the master of the calculated pause and the subtle facial expression, Tony Hancock was brilliantly served by his writers Alan Simpson and Ray Galton. In addition to the radio shows they wrote more than sixty television *Hancock's Half-Hours*, creating the faded gentility and humorous despair of Railway Cuttings, East Cheam. One of their finest scripts was written for the last BBC series – re-titled simply *Hancock* – and first transmitted on 23 June 1961. The two excerpts quoted here present the best-remembered confrontations from the show.

THE NURSE ....June Whitfield

THE DOCTOR ....Patrick Cargill

2ND NURSE..............................Anne Marryott

`The Blood Donor`

NURSE: Good afternoon, sir.

HANCOCK: Good afternoon, nurse. I've come in answer to your advert on the wall next to the Eagle Laundry in Pelham Road.

NURSE: An advert? Pelham Road?

HANCOCK: Yes. Your poster. You must have seen it – there's a nurse pointing at you, a Red Cross lady actually I believe, with a moustache and a beard . . . pencilled in, of course. You must know it – it's one of yours – it's next to 'Chamberlain Must Go', just above the cricket stumps. It says 'Your blood can save a life'.

NURSE: Oh, I see – you wish to become a blood donor.

HANCOCK: I certainly do. I've been thinking about this for a long time. No man is an island, young lady. To do one unselfish act with no thought of profit or gain is the duty of every human being. Something for the benefit of the country as a whole. What should it be, I thought – become a blood donor or join the Young Conservatives? But as I'm not looking for a wife and I can't play table-tennis, here I am – a body full of good British blood and raring to go.

NURSE: Yes, quite. Well now, would you sit down and I'll just take a few particulars. May I have your name?

HANCOCK: Yes, Hancock. Anthony Hancock. Twice candidate for the County Council elections, defeated; Hon. Sec. British Legion, Earls Court Branch; treasurer of the darts team and the outings committee.

NURSE: I only want the name.

HANCOCK: We're going to Margate this year – by boat – if there are any young nurses like yourself who would care to join us, we would be more than happy to accommodate you. No funny business – you know what I mean . . .

NURSE: Thank you, I'll bear it in mind. Now, date of birth?

HANCOCK: Er, yes, yes. Shall we say the twelfth of May, nineteen er . . . I always remember the twelfth of May – it was Coronation Day, you know, nineteen-thirty-six.

NURSE: You're only twenty-five?

HANCOCK: No, no, no, no – the Coronation was in nineteen-thirty-six – I was born a little before that in, er, nineteen er . . . is all this really necessary?

NURSE: Yes, I'm afraid so. The twelfth of May . . .

HANCOCK: Yes. I always remember that, the Coronation, we all got a day off at our school . . . did you? And we got a cup and saucer in a box and a bar of soap. Very good, I've still got that, and a spoon for the Silver Jubilee and a biscuit tin with their pictures on . . .

NURSE: *How old are you?*

HANCOCK *(disgruntled)*: Thirty-five.

NURSE: Thank you. Nationality?

HANCOCK: Ah, you've got nothing to worry about there. It's blood you're thinking about, isn't it. British. British. Undiluted for twelve generations. One hundred percent Anglo-Saxon, with perhaps just a touch of Viking, but nothing else has crept in. No, anybody who gets any of this will have nothing to complain about. There's aristocracy in there, you know. You want to watch who you're giving it to – it's like motor oil, it doesn't mix, if you get my meaning.

NURSE: Mr Hancock, when a blood transfusion is being given, the family background is of no consequence.

HANCOCK: Oh come now, surely you don't expect me to believe that. I mean, after all, east is east, really . . .

NURSE *(slightly needled)*: And blood is blood, Mr Hancock, the world over. It is classified by groups and not by accidents of birth.

HANCOCK: I did not come here for a lecture on Communism, young lady.

NURSE: I happen to be a Conservative.

HANCOCK: Then kindly behave like one, madam.

NURSE: Have you had any of these diseases?

(She hands him a printed list, which Hancock reads. He tries to remember a couple of the names on it; looks puzzled by one, then uncomfortable at another, then indignant at another.)

HANCOCK: How dare you. *(Starts to hand the list back.)* No I have not. *(Points.)* And especially that one. I told you before you have nothing to fear from me. I am perfectly healthy. Fit? Fit? If we'd had our own rocket, I'd've been the first one up there. I had my name down for Blue Streak, but no, we missed our chance again. It's not right having these foreigners hurtling round up there, you mark my words . . .

NURSE: Blood, Mr Hancock, blood.

HANCOCK: Eh? Yes. Ah, yes. I beg your pardon. I do get carried away over things like that – it's a sore point with me. *(Eager.)* Are we ready now, then?

NURSE: There is just one more thing. Have you given any blood before?

HANCOCK: Given, no. Spilt, yes. Yes, there's a good few drops lying about on the battlefields of Europe. Are you familiar with the Ardennes? *(Nurse looks up, startled.)* I well remember Von Runstedt's last push – Tiger Harrison and myself, being in a forward position, were cut off behind the enemy lines. 'Captain Harrison,' I said. 'Yes, sir,' he said. *(Nurse raises an eyebrow.)* 'Jerry's overlooked us,' I said. 'Where shall we head for?' 'Berlin,' he said. 'Right,' I said. 'Last one in the Reichstag is a sissy.' So we set off – got there three days before the Russians . . .

NURSE: You've never been a blood donor before.

HANCOCK: Yes. No. So – there we were, surrounded by Storm Troopers. 'Kamerad, Kamerad,' they said . . .

(The nurse has not taken any notice of this, and now hands him a card.)

NURSE: If you will just sit over there with the others, Doctor will call you when he's ready.

* * *

(The other nurse comes out.)

2ND NURSE: Well, Mr Hancock, Doctor is ready for you now.

HANCOCK: Who, me? Um . . . now? Yes, well, I mean is there . . . there's nobody else before me? I'm in no hurry. *(Looks round.)* Does anybody want to go in first?

2ND NURSE: There isn't anybody else, you're the last one.

HANCOCK: Oh. Yes. Well . . . this is it, then. *(To the first nurse.)* Over the top!

(They start towards the annexe where the doctor is waiting.)

HANCOCK *(confidential)*: What's he like on the needle, this bloke? Steady hand?

2ND NURSE: There's nothing to worry about.

HANCOCK: Is he in a good mood?

2ND NURSE: You'll be quite all right. Doctor MacTaggart is an excellent doctor.

HANCOCK: MacTaggart! He's a Scotsman! Ah well, that's all right. Marvellous doctors, the Scots, like their engineers, you know . . . It's the porridge that does it. Lead on, MacDuff!

(She leads him into the annexe where the doctor is sitting at a table. By him is all the paraphernalia required for blood

donations.)

2ND NURSE: Mr Hancock.

HANCOCK: Ah, guid morning, it's a braw bricht moonlicht nicht the morning, mista, it's a bonny wee lassie ye got there helping you, hoots mon . . . and och aye te ye the noo. . . .

DOCTOR *(educated English accent):* Would you mind sitting down there, Mr Hancock.

HANCOCK: Oh, I beg your pardon for lapsing into the vernacular, but the young lady did say you were a Scottish gentleman.

DOCTOR: Yes, well we're not all Rob Roys. May I have your card please?

HANCOCK: By all means. *(Sits down and hands his card to the doctor.)* I'm ready when you are, Squire.

DOCTOR *(looking at the card):* Good. Hold your hand out, please.

(Hancock holds his hand out. The Doctor cleans Hancock's thumb and then picks up the needle.)

DOCTOR: Now this won't hurt. You'll just feel a slight prick on the end of your thumb.

(Hancock winces in readiness, screwing his eyes shut. The doctor jabs the needle in. Hancock winces again, then has a look at the end of his thumb. He beams proudly.)

HANCOCK: Dear oh dear. Well, that's that. I'll have my cup of tea and biscuits now. Nothing to it, is there, really. I can't understand why everybody doesn't do it. *(Gets up.)* Well, I'll bid you good day, thank you very much. Whenever you want any more, don't hesitate to get in touch with me.

DOCTOR: Where are you going?

HANCOCK: To have my tea and biscuits.

DOCTOR: I thought you came here to give some of your blood.

HANCOCK: You've just had it.

DOCTOR: That is just a smear.

HANCOCK: It may be just a smear to you, mate, but it's life and death to some poor wretch.

DOCTOR: No, no, no – I've just taken a small sample to test.

HANCOCK: A sample? How much do you want, then?

DOCTOR: Well, a pint, of course.

HANCOCK: A *pint*? Have you gone raving mad? Oh well of course . . . I mean, you must be joking.

DOCTOR: A pint is a perfectly normal quantity to take.

HANCOCK: You don't seriously expect me to believe that? I mean, I came in here in all good faith to help my country. I don't mind giving a reasonable amount, but a pint . . . why, that's very nearly an armful. I'm sorry. I'm not walking round with an empty arm for anybody. I mean, a joke's a joke . . .

DOCTOR: Mr Hancock, obviously you don't know very much about the workings of the human body. You won't have an empty arm . . . or an empty anything. The blood is circulating all the time. A normal healthy individual can give a pint of blood without any ill effects whatsoever. You do have eight pints, you know.

HANCOCK: Now look, chum, everybody to his own trade, I'll grant you, but if I've got eight pints, obviously I *need* eight pints – and not seven, as I will have by the time you've finished with me. No, I'm sorry, I've been misinformed, I've made a mistake. I'll do something else. I'll be a Traffic Warden . . .

DOCTOR: Well, of course I can't force you to donate your blood, but it's a great shame. You're AB negative.

HANCOCK: Is that bad?

DOCTOR: Oh, no, no – you're rhesus positive.

HANCOCK: Rhesus? They're monkeys, aren't they? How dare you! What are you implying? I didn't come here to be insulted by a legalized vampire.

DOCTOR: Mr Hancock, that is your blood group. AB negative. It is one of the rarest groups there is.

HANCOCK *(pleased)*: Really?

DOCTOR: Yes, it is. Very rare indeed.

HANCOCK: Oh. Well, of course I'm not surprised. I've always felt instinctively that I was somehow different from the rest of the herd. Something apart. I never fitted into society – I've never belonged, if you know what I mean, the contact was never there. I was always a bit of an outsider. Well, that explains it. AB negative. One of Nature's aristocrats.

DOCTOR: I really think you ought to reconsider your decision.

HANCOCK: Yes, well of course this does throw a different complexion on the matter. Well I mean, if I am one of the few sources, one doesn't like to hog it all, so to speak. I'm not un-Christian. Very rare, eh?

DOCTOR: Yes, and I assure you there will be no ill effects. You'll make up the deficiency in no time at all.

HANCOCK: Oh well, in that case, I'll do it. I mean, we AB negatives must stick together. A minority group like us, we could be persecuted.

DOCTOR: Thank you very much, Mr Hancock, I'm most grateful. Now, if you would just take off your coat and lie down over there, it won't take very long. Afterwards you rest for half an hour and then you're free to go.

(Hancock lies down on the bed. The nurse wheels the apparatus over. Hancock watches apprehensively.)

DOCTOR: Just roll up your sleeve.
  (Hancock does so. The doctor starts preparing the apparatus, and then dabs Hancock's arm with cotton wool.)
HANCOCK: As a matter of interest, what group are you?
DOCTOR: Group A.
HANCOCK *(reacts disparagingly)*: Huh!
DOCTOR: Now, this won't hurt . . . relax . . .
  (Hancock tenses himself, relaxes at the command, then winces as the needle goes in, screwing his face up. He has a look down at his arm, and then turns his head away, feeling weak. He faints.)

THE MARX BROTHERS

The verbal highlights of the Marx Brothers' films tend to be the confrontations between Groucho and Chico. This one comes from the 1935 MGM film *A Night At The Opera*, written by George S. Kaufman and Morrie Ryskind. Groucho plays Otis B. Driftwood, and Chico plays Fiorello (not that it matters).

The Contract Scene from

`A Night at the Opera`

GROUCHO: Say, I just remembered – I came back here looking for somebody – you don't know who it is, do you?

CHICO: Is a funny thing, it just slipped my mind.

GROUCHO: Oh, I know – I know – the greatest tenor in the world, that's what I'm after.

CHICO: Why, I'm his manager.

GROUCHO: Who's manager?

CHICO: The greatest tenor in the world.

GROUCHO: The fellow who sings at the Opera here?

CHICO: Sure.

GROUCHO: What's his name?

CHICO: What do you care – I can't pronounce it. What do you want with him?

GROUCHO: Well, er – I want to sign him up for the New York Opera Company. You know that America is waiting to hear him sing?

CHICO: Well, he can sing loud, but he can't sing *that* loud.

GROUCHO: Well I think I can get America to meet him half-way. Could he sail tomorrow?

CHICO: You pay him enough money he could sail yesterday. How much you pay him?

GROUCHO: Well, I don't know – let's see . . . *(To himself:)* A thousand dollars a night – I'm entitled to a small profit . . . *(To Chico:)* How about ten dollars a night?

CHICO: Ten dollars . . . *(laughs derisively)* . . . I'll take it.

GROUCHO: All right, but remember I get ten percent for negotiating the deal.

CHICO: Yes, and I get ten percent for being the manager. How much does that leave?

GROUCHO: Well, that leaves him, er – eight dollars.

CHICO: Eight dollars, eh? Well, he sends five dollars home to his mother . . .

GROUCHO: Well, that leaves three dollars.

CHICO: Can he live in New York on three dollars?

GROUCHO: Like a prince. Of course he won't be able to eat, but he can live like a prince. However, out of that three dollars, you know, he'll have to pay an income tax.

CHICO: Oh, income tax.

GROUCHO: Yes, you know there's a Federal tax, and a State tax, and a City tax, and a street tax, and a sewer tax.

CHICO: How much does this come to?

GROUCHO: Well, I figure if he doesn't sing too often he can break even.

CHICO: All right, we take it.

GROUCHO: All right, fine. Now, here are the contracts. You just put his name at the top, and you sign at the bottom. There's no need of you reading that, because these are duplicates.

CHICO *(looking at his copy)*: Is a duplicate, yes . . .

GROUCHO: I say they're duplicates . . . don't you know what duplicates are?

CHICO: Sure, there's five kids up in Canada.*

GROUCHO: Well I wouldn't know about that – I haven't been in Canada in years. Well go ahead and read it.

CHICO: What does it say?

GROUCHO: Well go on and read it.

CHICO: You read it.

GROUCHO: All right, I'll read it to you. Can you hear?

CHICO: I haven't heard anything yet. D'you say anything?

GROUCHO: Well I haven't said anything worth hearing.

CHICO: Well that's why I didn't hear anything.

GROUCHO: Well that's why I didn't say anything.

---

* The Dionne quintuplets.

CHICO: Can *you* read?

GROUCHO: I can read, but I can't see it. Don't seem to have it in focus here . . . if my arms were a little longer I could read it . . . you haven't got a baboon in your pocket have you? Here, here, here we are, now I've got it. Now pay particular attention to this first clause because it's most important. It says, 'The party of the first part shall be known in this contract as the party of the first part'. How do you like that, that's pretty neat, eh?

CHICO: No, that's no good.

GROUCHO: What's the matter with it?

CHICO: I don't know – let's hear it again.

GROUCHO: It says, 'The party of the first part shall be known in this contract as the party of the first part'.

CHICO: It sounds a little better this time.

GROUCHO: Well, it grows on you. Would you like to hear it once more?

CHICO: Just the first part.

GROUCHO: What do you mean, the party of the first part?

CHICO: No, the first part of the party of the first part.

GROUCHO: All right – it says 'the first part of the party of the first part shall be known in this contract as the first part of the party of the first part shall be known in this contract . . .' look, why should we quarrel about a thing like this, we'll take it right out, eh?

CHICO: It's-a too long anyhow.

(They each tear off the top of their copies of the contract.)

CHICO: Now what have we got left?

GROUCHO: Well, I got about a foot and a half. Now it says, 'the party of the second part shall be known in this contract as the party of the second part'.

CHICO: Well, I don't know about that.

GROUCHO: *Now* what's the matter?

CHICO: I don't like-a the second party either.

GROUCHO: Well, you should have come to the first party, we didn't get home till around four in the morning. I was blind for three days.

CHICO: Hey, look – why can't-a the first part of the second party be the second part of the first party – then you got something.

GROUCHO: Well look, er – rather than go through all that again, what do you say?

CHICO: Fine.

(They each tear it off their contracts.)

GROUCHO: Now I've got something here you're bound to like – you'll be crazy about it.

CHICO: No, I don't like it.

GROUCHO: You don't like *what*?

CHICO: Whatever it is, I don't like it.

GROUCHO: Well, don't let's break up an old friendship over a thing like that – ready?

CHICO: O.K.

(They tear it off their contracts.)

CHICO: Now the next part I don't think you're going to like.

GROUCHO: Well, your word's good enough for me.

(They tear the next section off the contracts.)

GROUCHO: Now then, is my word good enough for you?

CHICO: I should say not.

GROUCHO: Well, that takes out two more clauses.

(They tear off the next two clauses.)

GROUCHO: Now, the party of the eighth part . . .

CHICO: No, that's no good, no.

(They tear it off.)

GROUCHO: The party of the ninth part . . .

CHICO: No, that's no good, too.

(They tear it off. Chico has by now torn more off his contract than Groucho.)

CHICO: Hey, how is it my contract is skinnier than yours?

GROUCHO: Well, I don't know – you must have been out on a tear last night. But anyhow, we're all set now, aren't we?

CHICO: Sure.

GROUCHO: Now just you put your name right down just there and then the deal is legal.

CHICO: Hey, I forgot to tell you, I can't write.

GROUCHO: Oh, that's all right – there's no ink in the pen anyhow. But listen – it's a contract, isn't it?

CHICO: Oh, sure.

GROUCHO: We got a contract, no matter how small it is.

CHICO: Hey, wait, wait . . . what does this say, here, this thing here?

GROUCHO: That? Oh, that's the usual clause – that's in every contract. That just says, it says, 'If any of the parties participating in this contract are shown not to be in their right minds the entire agreement is automatically nullified'.

CHICO: Well, I don't know . . .

GROUCHO: It's all right, that's in every contract – that's what they call a Sanity Clause.

CHICO *(laughs)*: You can't fool me – there ain't no Sanity-Claus.

`MONTY PYTHON'S FLYING CIRCUS`

The team of John Cleese, Graham Chapman, Terry Jones, Michael Palin, Eric Idle and animator Terry Gilliam did for (or to) television comedy what *The Goon Show* had done for radio. Of all their sketches, the most often quoted is Cleese and Palin's confrontation in a pet shop (first broadcast on BBC-1 on 7 December 1969) – perhaps the most famous consumer complaint since the passing of the Trades Descriptions Act.

`Parrot`

CLEESE *(entering shop with a dead parrot in a cage)*: Hallo, I wish to register a complaint . . . Hallo – miss?

PALIN: What do you mean, 'miss'?

CLEESE: Oh, I'm sorry – I have a cold. I wish to make a complaint.

PALIN: Sorry, we're closing for lunch.

CLEESE: Never mind that, my lad, I wish to complain about this parrot what I purchased not half an hour ago from this very boutique.

PALIN: Oh yes, the Norwegian Blue – what's wrong with it?

CLEESE: I'll tell you what's wrong with it – it's dead, that's what's wrong with it.

PALIN: No, no – it's resting, look . . .

CLEESE: Look, my lad, I know a dead parrot when I see one, and I'm looking at one right now.

PALIN: No, no – it's not dead, it's resting.

CLEESE: *Resting*?

PALIN: Yes. Remarkable bird, the Norwegian Blue. Beautiful plumage, ain't it?

CLEESE: The plumage don't enter into it – it's stone dead.

PALIN: No, no – it's resting.

CLEESE: All right then – if it's resting I'll wake it up. *(Shouts into cage.)* Hallo, Polly! I got a nice cuttlefish for you when you wake up, Polly Parrot!

PALIN *(jogging cage)*: There, it moved.

CLEESE: No it didn't! That was you pushing the cage!

PALIN: I did not!

CLEESE: Yes you did! *(Takes parrot out of cage.)* Hallo Polly! *(Shouting in its ear.)* PO-LLY! PO-LLY! *(Bangs it against counter.)* Polly parrot – wake up! PO-LLY! *(Throws it in the air and lets it fall to the floor.)* Now that's what I call a dead parrot.

PALIN: No, no – it's stunned.

CLEESE: Look, my lad – I've had just about enough of this! That parrot is definitely deceased! And when I bought it not half an hour ago, you assured me that its lack of movement was due to it being tired and shagged out after a long squawk.

PALIN: It's probably pining for the fiords.

CLEESE: Pining for the fiords – what kind of talk is that? Look, why did it fall flat on its back the moment I got it home?

PALIN: The Norwegian Blue prefers kipping on its back. It's a beautiful bird – lovely plumage . . .

CLEESE: Look, I took the liberty of examining that parrot, and I discovered that the only reason it had been sitting on its perch in the first place was that it had been nailed there.

PALIN: 'Course it was nailed there, otherwise it would have muscled up to those bars and voom!

CLEESE: Look, matey, this parrot wouldn't 'voom' if I put four thousand volts through it. It's bleeding demised.

PALIN: It's not – it's pining!

CLEESE: It's *not* pining – it's passed on! This parrot is no more! It has ceased to be! It's expired and gone to meet its maker! This is a late parrot! It's a stiff! Bereft of life it rests in peace – if you hadn't nailed it to the perch it would be pushing up the daisies! It's rung down the curtain and joined the choir invisible! THIS IS AN EX-PARROT!

MORECAMBE AND WISE

Eric Morecambe and Ernie Wise began their double-act as teenagers, and rose from being a very third-rate act to the position of best-loved and highest-paid performers on British television. They were superbly served by their writer for the BBC series, Eddie Braben, who developed their characters from the simple straight man and comic into something more complex: Morecambe once said, 'The premise is, he's an idiot, but I'm a bigger idiot'. This sketch was first broadcast on 16 February 1973, and gave them one of their catch-phrases.

`Mr Memory`

ERNIE: And now ladies and gentlemen it's with great pleasure I would like to introduce to you now that great international star – from the Continent, and Europe – the fantastic, the world-famous – Mr Memory!

(Applause. The orchestra plays 'Thanks for the Memory'. Enter Eric.)

ERNIE: Thank you, thank you – good evening, Mr Memory.

ERIC: Good morning.

ERNIE: Mr Memory, I understand that you have a brain capable of remembering every event that ever happened anywhere at any time in the world.

ERIC: That is correct.

ERNIE: Question number one, Mr Memory – could you please tell me who won the F.A. Cup in nineteen-hundred-and-fifty?

ERIC: F.A. Cup, nineteen-hundred-and-fifty.

ERNIE: Yes. *(Produces a cough that sounds suspiciously like 'Arsenal'.)*

ERIC *(triumphantly)*: Tranmere Rovers! . . . No?

ERNIE: No.

ERIC: No, no – no, it was not Tranmere Rovers . . .

ERNIE: No.

ERIC: . . . That was just additional information thrown in just for your benefit. Quite free.

ERNIE: *(Coughs 'Arsenal' again.)*

ERIC: It was, er . . .

ERNIE *(coughs, as above)*: . . . Excuse me, I've got a very chesty cold, here.

ERIC: (Thank you) . . . It was . . . Chester! Chester won the F.A. Cup in nineteen-fifty!

ERNIE: No! *(Coughs again.)*

ERIC *(promptly)*: Arsenal! – won the F.A. Cup in nineteen-fifty as well!

ERNIE: Absolutely correct.

ERIC: And the man who scored the goal had a nasty cough.

ERNIE: Congratulations, Mr Memory.

ERIC: Thank you.

ERNIE: Now, could you please tell me, who was the English Prime Minister, in England . . .

ERIC: That's clever! . . .

ERNIE: . . . in 1801?

ERIC: The English Prime Minister . . . in England . . .

BOTH: . . . in 1801.

ERNIE *(nudges Eric)*: Whoops! Sorry – you nearly fell down that big deep pit, William.

ERIC: The English Prime Minister, of England, in 1801, was William Big!

ERNIE: No! Think again.

ERIC: William Deep!

ERNIE: No!

ERIC: William Pitt!

ERNIE: Absolutely correct!

ERIC: Thank you.

ERNIE *(clears his throat.)*

ERIC: Arsenal!

ERNIE: Now – for question number three. Could you tell me, who was it who formed the British Police Force?

ERIC: Oh, I'm often asked this.

ERNIE: Well?

ERIC: Yes, thank you.

ERNIE: Why, it's easy. Of course it's easy – it's as easy as peeling – as *peeling* – an orange.

ERIC: Ladies and gentlemen – the British Police Force was formed by Sir Max Jaffa!

ERNIE: No!! But – the 'Sir' part was right . . .

ERIC: Sir Nell Gwynn!

ERNIE: No – not quite correct.

ERIC: Sir Not Quite Correct?

ERNIE: No, no – I ap*peal* to you!

ERIC: Sir Robert Peel! Sir Robert Peel – formed – Sir Max Jaffa!

ERNIE: No – the British Police Force.

ERIC: As well.

ERNIE: Absolutely correct!

ERIC: Yes!

ERNIE *(clears his throat.)*

ERIC: Arsenal!

ERNIE: Congratulations, sir. That was absolutely brilliant. They're absolutely non-plussed out there.

ERIC: I'm sure they are!

ERNIE: They can't believe it ever happened.

ERIC: Well, can I have my money now?

ERNIE: You'd like a rest in the dressing-room?

ERIC: Well, I've worked very hard.

ERNIE: Of course you have, your brain must be tired.

ERIC: It's going round.

ERNIE: All the time . . . well, here's your money *(hands Eric some notes)* . . . it was agreed, five pounds, wasn't it?

ERIC: No?

ERNIE: Yes, it was five pounds.

ERIC: No – it was ten.

ERNIE: Please – it was five pounds.

ERIC: Ten pounds.

ERNIE: It was definitely five pounds!

ERIC: Well, you could be right, I've got a shocking memory. *(They move upstage. Ernie clears his throat.)*

ERIC: Arsenal!

`STEPTOE AND SON`

Alan Simpson and Ray Galton made their name as Tony Hancock's scriptwriters; their first essay into writing away from Hancock was a series of different half-hour plays under the title *Comedy Playhouse*. One of them was so successful that it led to the long-running series about the junk-men Albert Steptoe and his son Harold. The original programme – quoted complete here – is remarkable for the depth of the characters; very little needed to be added to them as the series progressed. The first broadcast was on BBC-TV on 5 January 1961.

ALBERT STEPTOE......................Wilfrid Brambell
HAROLD STEPTOE....................Harry H. Corbett

`The Offer`

Open on film clip, as Harold drives the horse and cart down the street and turns into the yard. The yard itself leads to the stable and the house, a broken-down mews-type building. Albert (Harold's father) and Harold unhitch the horse and lead it into the stable. Dissolve to studio set of the yard. Albert is sorting through the junk on the cart.

ALBERT: What's all this, then. Have you been out all day just for this? All day just to collect this load of rubbish.

HAROLD: For Gawd's sake don't start, Dad.

ALBERT: Where's the lead? I told you specially to keep your eye out for lead.

HAROLD: There ain't no lead about.

ALBERT: Where's the brass — there ain't no brass here.

HAROLD: There ain't no brass about either.

ALBERT: Of course there's brass about. There's always brass about — and lead. You got to shout for it. If it ain't tied up in ribbons out by the front gate you don't want to know, do you. Go and feed the horse.

HAROLD: I'm going to. *(Starts unhooking the nosebag.)* What do you think I'm unhooking the nosebag for?

ALBERT: And that's another thing, you don't treat that horse proper. How can you expect to get round quick if the horse ain't in good nick?

HAROLD: Look, you look after the yard, I'll look after the horse and cart, all right?

ALBERT: He don't get enough to eat. He's entitled to eat, that horse, same as you and me are.

HAROLD: For Gawd's sake don't keep on about that horse.

ALBERT: He's a dumb animal, he can't say when he's hungry.

HAROLD: Well this one can, the great greedy hungry-gutted clodhopper . . .

ALBERT: You mind your language. Your mother didn't like it,

no more do I. You didn't pick it off of us, so don't you come out with it.

HAROLD: The greedy hungry-gutted great clodhopping . . . 'stop at their houses' – I daren't stop – I get off and knock on a door, by the time they've opened it he's got half their hedge inside him.

ALBERT: Come on, give us a hand down with this rubbish.

HAROLD: I was going to feed the horse.

ALBERT: Leave the horse, this is more important. Give us a hand down with this chaise-longue.

(They get the chaise-longue off the cart. The seat is half missing, with bits of straw hanging out.)

ALBERT: What good's this – look at it, what good is it!

HAROLD: That's your precious horse done that. I had it down on the pavement, went in to pay the woman, and old greedy guts had his choppers stuck into it. He's useless, I'm telling you – he's old, and he's slow – I don't know, why you don't take him round the knacker's yard and have him melted down.

ALBERT: You don't like that horse, do you. Come on, admit it, you never have liked him, have you?

HAROLD: Well, now you've brought it up – no I don't. He's vicious. He lunged at me again today.

ALBERT *(laughs)*: He's no fool . . . he know's when he's not liked. You don't know how to handle him proper like I do. He don't lunge at me.

HAROLD: 'Course he don't, not the way you treat him, giving him sweets and lumps of sugar all the time. His teeth have gone rotten through you. I don't call that being kind to a horse, making his teeth go rotten.

ALBERT: It's not the sweets, he's getting old. That's why his teeth's rotten.

HAROLD: He's rotten all over. Glue, that's all he's good for.
(Albert picks up a bundle of old clothes and weighs them.)

ALBERT: What's this — woollens or rags?

HAROLD: Bit of both.

ALBERT: What *rates* did you pay, woollens or rags? You got
six pounds here — is it cream or dark?

HAROLD: Mostly cream, the rest is dark.

ALBERT: What sort of a totter are you — how many times have
I told you to sort 'em out before you pay for 'em.

HAROLD: Gordon Bennett — I only give her a tanner for the
lot!

ALBERT: Oh . . . well, that's not bad, I suppose. But sort them
out next time.

HAROLD *(annoyed)*: Here, look — you moan about the way I
treat the horse, you moan about the way I got out totting
. . . *you* go out — go on — I don't mind staying here in the
yard, sitting round the fire drinking cups of tea all day
long . . . go on, you get up on the plank, you're so good at
it . . . I'm sick and tired of sitting up there watching that
great backside all day long. You go out tomorrow.

ALBERT: You know I can't get out in the cart no more, with
my legs.

HAROLD: Yeah, well, that's it then, ain't it . . . you don't
want to say nothing, do you, otherwise I'll jack this lot in
and be off. I'm sick and tired of you, and the yard, and the
horse, and the cart.

ALBERT: Yeah — what do *you* know — what could *you* do?

HAROLD: Don't worry about me, mate — I'll be all right — I've
had an offer.

ALBERT: Get out of it.

HAROLD: Oh yes I have. And it don't include you or your
rotten horse. See? OK? All right? Well, watch it.

(Pause.)

ALBERT: What offer? Who from?

HAROLD: Never you mind. I'll go and feed the horse.

ALBERT: You don't want to go taking no offers, we've got a good business here.

HAROLD: You're worried now, ain't you.

ALBERT: You don't want to go taking no offers. Young fellow like you – there's not many fellows of your age has a partnership in a thriving business like this one.

HAROLD: I'm thirty-seven, dad.

ALBERT: Well, that's young, ain't it? I'm telling you, if *I* was thirty-seven *I'd* be out there behind that horse.

HAROLD: If you were thirty-seven you wouldn't be out with that horse, because that horse wouldn't have been born. You would have been out with the horse we had before, and it was a damn sight better horse than the rotten thing I have to go round with.

ALBERT: That's right, blame the horse – a bad workman always blames his tools. You've had it too easy, you have. My dad made me come up the hard way, that's where I gone wrong. You didn't have to work your way up – straight into the business you came, with your own cart – and your own horse. And your name on the gate.

HAROLD: My name ain't on the gate . . . it's got 'and Son'.

ALBERT: That's you, ain't it?

HAROLD: No it ain't – it's you. Your dad had that sign painted.

ALBERT: Yeah, well, it's an old firm, there's no point in wasting money keeping painting the sign. It'll be all yours one day, when I'm dead and buried . . . and I don't suppose that'll be very long . . .

HAROLD: Oh, Gawd, here we go. . . .

(He grabs an old stringless violin off the cart.)

HAROLD: Here – a quick chorus of 'Hearts and Flowers', all right? *(Starts la-la-ing the tune and pretending to play the violin.)* Come on, then . . . come on . . . come on, tell us how you're hard done by. Tell us how ill you are. Come on . . . Tell us how you worked your fingers to the bone – come on – and how ungrateful I am . . .

ALBERT: You stop that . . . stop it, do you hear . . .
(He looks about for a weapon. Harold is enjoying it now and keeps la-la-ing 'Hearts and Flowers'. Albert in a temper grabs a sword in a scabbard off a pile of junk.)

ALBERT *(waving it about)*: . . . or I'll have your head off!
(Harold is now holding the violin as a weapon, and laughing at the old man.)

HAROLD: You want to take it out of the scabbard first, don't you.
(Albert tries vainly to get the sword out of the scabbard. It won't come. He gets into a paddy but it still won't budge. He throws it away, and leans exhausted against the cart, holding his heart.)

ALBERT: Oooh . . . ooh . . . help . . . it's me heart, it's started again . . . I think I've overdone it this time.

HAROLD: There's nothing wrong with you.

ALBERT: It's me heart I tell you.

HAROLD: You been moaning about your heart for forty years – every time you can't get your own way. You've had fifteen heart attacks to my knowledge . . . and if you have three you *die*.

ALBERT: Who told you that?

HAROLD: The doctor who come here before – he says there's nothing wrong with you, anywhere.

ALBERT: He's lying – there's me legs.

HAROLD: There was nothing wrong with your legs just now, was there – when you was jumping about, when you was going to have my head off. Come on, let's finish unloading the gear.

(They continue unloading the cart.)

ALBERT: You don't want to go taking no offers, son. I've built this business up for you. It'll be yours when I'm gone. Then when your son comes along, you won't have to change the sign either . . . 'Steptoe and Son', only it'll be you and your son.

HAROLD: But I ain't got a son, have I. I ain't even got a wife.

ALBERT: Well go out and get one.

HAROLD: Look, dad, I'm not going to get married. Every time I meet a bird and she says to me what do I do and I say I'm a rag and bone man, she don't want to know.

ALBERT *(indignant)*: And what's wrong with rag and bone men? It's an honourable profession. Very useful members of the community we are. You tell them that next time they start turning their noses up. *(Poking a mattress on the cart.)* That's not bad – where did you get that?

HAROLD: Oh, some old bird in Devlin Street. She wanted half a dollar for it, saucy old moo.

ALBERT: You didn't give it to her.

HAROLD: No, 'course not. In the end she gave me three and a tanner to take it away.

ALBERT *(cackles)*: You're learning, son. You're not such a rotten rag and bone man. *(Walking up and down on the mattress.)* It's not bad, is it – good quality. Not many lumps in it. Look – it's still got the Utility sign on it. I'll have that for my bed. When you fed the horse, bring mine down and bring this up.

HAROLD: All right. I'll get you a continental headboard and a bedside cabinet if you'd like to hang on.

ALBERT: Don't be saucy.

HAROLD: Well — if anything half decent comes along, you want to keep it for yourself, don't you. That's no way to run a business. All the time you want to, be taking everything we've got — you're like a little old squirrel, you are — with all your nuts all hidden away for the winter.

ALBERT: I'm only trying to build up a decent home for you. You don't want your wife coming back into a slum, do you? What's this?

(He holds up a plate with a chunk chipped out of it.)

HAROLD: What's it look like — it's a plate.

ALBERT: Look nice on the wall, that would.

HAROLD: What do you want to put it on the wall for? They're to eat off of. That's the idea of them. You wouldn't put wallpaper on the table, would you? I don't know what's the matter with you — I think you're going potty in your old age.

ALBERT: This is going on my wall.

HAROLD: Look, I thought the idea of this game was to collect the gear and flog it — you never want to flog nothing, do you — you want to keep everything for yourself.

ALBERT: You can't go flogging things like this. Look at it — it's beautiful. Look at that glaze. It's the finest piece of Crown Derby that's ever came into the yard.

HAROLD: Crown Derby . . . your eyes is going. That's Red Anchor Chelsea, that is.

ALBERT: Never. What do *you* know about pottery.

HAROLD: That's Red Anchor Chelsea — I'm telling you.

ALBERT: Never.

HAROLD: I had you over that Chinese vase, didn't I — I proved you wrong there.

ALBERT: What vase?

HAROLD: That Ming Dynasty. The one you keep your threepenny bits in. You said it was a Tang Dynasty.

ALBERT: Well, so it is.

HAROLD: It ain't, I tell you. It's a Ming Dynasty. I would have understood it if you'd thought it was a Sung Dynasty – but getting a Ming mixed up with a Tang! There's hundreds of years difference. Well, it just exposes you.

ALBERT: I'm sticking this up on my wall.

HAROLD: Oh, stick it where you like. I'm going to feed the horse.

ALBERT: Haven't you fed that poor animal yet?

HAROLD: Oh, don't start that again. And leave this junk on the waggon. That's for flogging. You've already had the plate and the mattress, now leave it alone. Leave it all out here – otherwise I'll take that offer.

(Harold wanders off with the nosebag. As he goes he takes a handful of oats out of the bag and samples them. Albert waits till he's gone and quickly rummages around the cart. He holds up an ornate gilt mirror with a large crack across it. He looks in it – poses a bit.)

ALBERT: That would look nice on the wall.

(He has a close look at his teeth.)

ALBERT: Well my choppers is all right, and I eat sweets.

(He looks round furtively to see if Harold is watching him, then slides the mirror under his coat. Fade out.)

Fade up the main room in the house, which is packed with statuettes, bric-a-brac, furniture, and a row of drink bottles with various amounts of liquid in. Albert is banging a couple of nails into the only part of the wall with nothing on it. He hangs up the chipped plate, and then takes a barometer out of a box by his side and hangs it up on the second nail. He goes to the window, looks at the weather, goes back and taps the barometer. As Harold comes in, Albert quickly moves a wardrobe to cover the barometer. Harold is carrying a boxful of booze bottles.

HAROLD: What have you been doing?

ALBERT: Nothing.

HAROLD: What was that banging I heard?

ALBERT: I didn't hear no banging. *(Looks round.)*

HAROLD: Have you been putting anything up on the wall?

ALBERT: No.

HAROLD: I distinctly heard banging. *(Looks round the room suspiciously.)*

ALBERT: Oh, banging – yes – I just been hanging up me old plate – me Crown Derby.

HAROLD: Red Anchor.

ALBERT: Yeah. Looks all right, don't it.

HAROLD *(putting the box of bottles down)*: You didn't take these off the cart, did you – you left these for me to bring in, didn't you.

ALBERT: It's me legs . . . you know.

HAROLD: Come on, help me sort these out. *(He sits down and takes a whisky bottle out of the box, holds it up – there is a tiny amount of liquid in it – and sniffs it.)* Whisky.

ALBERT: Whisky . . . Whisky . . . *(He goes to the shelf of bottles, looks along them until he comes to the one with whisky in it, takes it down and gives it to Harold.)* Here we are.

(Harold puts a funnel into the top of it, and pours the small amount of whisky from the first bottle into it. He shakes the funnel. He hands the full bottle back to Albert, who puts the

*cork in and returns it to the shelf. Harold takes a wine bottle
and looks at the label.)*

HAROLD: Chateau Margaux. We got any Chateau Margaux
up there?

(Albert looks along the shelf.)

ALBERT: Chateau Margaux . . . what year?

HAROLD: 1955.

ALBERT: Chateau Margaux 1955 . . . here we are.

*(He hands Harold a wine bottle from the shelf. Harold puts
the funnel in it and pours the remains of the first bottle into
it.)*

ALBERT: That's full up now.

HAROLD: Well – you know what to do – hammer the cork in
and lay it on its side.

ALBERT: Let's have a drop now.

HAROLD: No.

ALBERT: Oh, go on, let's have a drop now.

HAROLD: No – that's for when we got guests.

ALBERT: We don't have guests. It'll go rotten, I tell you – let's
drink it now.

HAROLD: We're not going to open it – we're not touching that
bottle . . . how can I build up a wine cellar if you want to
keep drinking it all. *(Looking at another bottle.)* How are
we off for Yugoslavian Riesling?

ALBERT: We don't have none.

HAROLD: Right, well take that and put it on the shelf. We'll
start a new bottle. *(Looking at another bottle.)* Non-vintage
Beaujolais.

ALBERT: Yeah, here you are. *(Hands him a bottle.)* Nearly full,
that one.

HAROLD: Good, this should finish it off.

(He pours the first bottle into the one from the shelf, then

sniffs it, then puts the neck of the empty bottle to his nose.)

ALBERT: What's the matter?

HAROLD: The rotten, lousy, stinking gits . . . paraffin! They put paraffin in it. Ruined me bottle of Beaujolais. Taken me a year to fill that up.

ALBERT: Told you we should have drunk it.

HAROLD: How can people do things like that.

ALBERT: Perhaps it won't matter. Taste it. I knew a man who drank methylated spirits. He swore by it.

HAROLD: Look – I'm not an alcoholic, mate – I'm a connoisseur.

ALBERT: Well, if you don't want it, I'll have it. I don't mind a drop of paraffin.

HAROLD: Ugh . . . you dirty old man . . .

(Albert takes a great long swig, then wipes his mouth with the back of his hand.)

ALBERT: Cor . . . lovely. You can hardly taste it. Here – have some.

HAROLD: Take that thing away from me. I'm not ruining my palate on that. You got no taste, have you? You're dead uncouth. How you ever had me I don't know, we're so different from each other.

ALBERT: Yeah, well you take after your mum – very respectable, she was – a schoolteacher before I married her . . . not after. I soon knocked that on the head. And another thing – it ain't the sweets that makes the horse's teeth go rotten. I been looking at mine – I eat more sweets than he does, and my teeth ain't rotten.

HAROLD: Well of course not – you got false teeth, haven't you. False teeth don't go rotten, do they.

ALBERT: Don't they?

HAROLD: 'Course they don't.

ALBERT: Oh. Perhaps we ought to get that horse some false teeth, then.

HAROLD: Melt him down, that's all he's good for . . . go on, take that thing away from me . . . *(Takes another bottle.)* Gin. Bring the gin over.

ALBERT: Gin. *(Gives him the gin bottle from the shelf.)*

HAROLD: And get us a bit of clean rag.

ALBERT: What for?

HAROLD: To wipe the funnel out, of course. I have been pouring red wine into that, haven't I. I don't want to pour gin on top of it, do I. It'll go pink, won't it. Ready with that bottle. *(He looks at the full gin bottle.)* Hallo, hallo – there was more than this in that.

ALBERT: Eh?

HAROLD: I said there was more than this in that.

ALBERT: Well don't look at me.

HAROLD: I *am* looking at you. I put a mark on this label, see. That's where the mark is, and that's where the gin is . . . two inches underneath it.

ALBERT: It must have evaporated.

HAROLD: Yeah, and I know where to. You been at it, ain't you? I been out on the cart and you been at the gin. Well, that's it, that's put the tin hat on it, that has – that's finished it, that's final – I'm going to take that offer.

ALBERT: I only had a little drop to keep the cold out – my legs was playing me up.

HAROLD: That's finished it, that has. I'm not putting up with that. I've had enough. That's one thing I'm not standing for, nicking stuff out of my cocktail cabinet.

(He starts to pack his bottles of liquor into the box.)

HAROLD: You gone too far this time. This is final. I'm going to pack everything on the horse and cart – I'm going to take that offer.

ALBERT: Harold, wait a minute – you can't leave me here all by myself – I'm too old to go on with it alone – Harold – you don't need taking no offer – you'll feel different in the morning, Harold, you've had a hard day. . . . .

HAROLD: Mind out of my way. I've made up my mind – I should have done this years ago. Mind out.

(He picks up the box and walks out into the yard and over to the cart. Albert scurries behind him.)

ALBERT: Harold – I won't touch your cocktail cabinet no more – don't leave me, son . . . I'll give you the plate. You can have the plate.

HAROLD *(by now back in the room)*: I don't want the plate. *(He starts grabbing things.)* I'm going to sell my share of this stuff, and I'm going to buy my way in, and I'll be away, see . . .

ALBERT: But what's going to happen to me? I'm too old to be left alone. *(Clutching his heart.)* Oooh – it's my heart – it's started again . . . Harold . . . I'm going, do you hear me, Harold, I'm going.

HAROLD: Well that makes two of us, don't it.

(He goes out to the cart again. Albert watches Harold go, then starts moaning when Harold comes back in.)

ALBERT: It's my heart – I'm on my way out . . .

HAROLD: Where's my barometer?

ALBERT: What barometer?

HAROLD: The one I bought today. Where is it?

ALBERT: I ain't seen no barometer.

(Harold moves the wardrobe and reveals the barometer.)

HAROLD: What's this, then – a banjo?

ALBERT: Don't take the barometer, Harold – I've always wanted a barometer.

HAROLD: It's mine. I can get a few bob on that. *(Takes it down.)*

ALBERT: It's no good to you. It's in French. You don't know what the French for cloudy is.

HAROLD: I don't have to know what the French for cloudy is, do I – I can look out of the window, can't I.

ALBERT: Then what do you want a barometer for?

HAROLD: I'm going to flog it. I'm going to flog all this gear, and buy my way in. Then I'll be away, see – I'll make a name for myself. I'll never make a name for myself here. Here I'm just 'and Son'. *(He picks up a couple of chairs and goes out into the yard. Albert follows him.)*

ALBERT: You don't want to go doing nothing you'll regret later.

(Harold throws the barometer and chairs onto the cart.)

HAROLD: Stop following me about.

ALBERT: I'm not following you about. It's my yard. I've a perfect right to walk if I want – I don't have to ask you.

HAROLD: Go on, then – walk up and down. *(Leans against the cart.)* Go on . . . go on, walk about then – I'll stop here.

ALBERT: I don't want to walk about.

HAROLD: No, you just want to follow me, don't you?

ALBERT: I don't want to follow you.

(Harold walks towards the room. Albert follows him. Harold stops and turns.)

HAROLD: See, you're following me.

(Harold changes direction a couple of times, then walks round the cart. The old man follows him. Harold finally makes for the room, and stops at the door.)

HAROLD: It ain't going to do you no good following me. I ain't going to change my mind. I'm off.

(He goes into the room and starts collecting more odds and

ends. Albert follows him in.)

ALBERT: So you've made up your mind, have you?

HAROLD: Yes I have. I've got a full life in front of me. I could have been a company director by now, but you've held me back all these years – you and that rotten horse, and that cart – keeping me all the time back – well, I'm breaking away, see – I'm going to strike out on my own. I'm going to make me mark and you ain't going to stop me – believe me, mate, Harold Steptoe's going *up*!

(He takes the stuff he's collected out and throws it on the cart, then goes back into the room. Albert follows him. Harold takes the wardrobe and tries to get it on his back.)

HAROLD: Give us a hand with this.

ALBERT: You mind you don't hurt yourself doing that . . . it's a rotten operation, that is, if you have it . . .

(Albert finds the barometer and whips it under his overcoat. Harold has got the wardrobe on the cart, looks round and spots a tatty armchair.)

HAROLD: Oh yes, that'll look very nice in my study, that will. I think I'll have it re-covered in red leather, with brass nails all round it . . . *(Puts the armchair on the cart.)* . . . a pine panelled library, I'll have – the books right up to the ceiling . . . me books, where's me books?

(He goes back into the room. Albert takes the barometer out from under his coat, puts it down and puts a tarpaulin over it. Harold re-appears with some books and an old golf bag with one club in it.)

ALBERT: You'll be playing a bit of golf, then, will you?

HAROLD: Oh yes, that's essential, that is – all company directors play golf. That's where all the big deals are done, on the golf course – you got to play golf. *(Picks up some old motor tyres.)* I'm taking these and all. Spare tyres for me motor car.

ALBERT: There's an old battery here.

HAROLD: Yeah, that's mine, and all. I'll keep it in my garage – my chauffeur can look after it. Bung it on. *(Albert does so.)* If there's anything else I need, I'll come back and get it. Well : . . that's it, then – I'll be off. Go and get the horse.

ALBERT: You're not having the horse.

HAROLD: I want the horse.

ALBERT: No – it's my horse, I'm not giving him to you.

HAROLD: I only want to borrow him, to get my stuff moved out.

ALBERT: No. You've never liked him, have you. You've never had a good word to say for him all the time we've had him.

HAROLD: I got to have the horse, otherwise how am I going to move my stuff out?

ALBERT: That's *your* problem, isn't it. You're not having the horse.

HAROLD: Keep your rotten stinking horse. It don't bother me, mate. I never got nothing in the past from you, so don't do me no favours, I don't want none now. That don't bother me – I'll soon have that on the move.

(Harold gets in between the shafts and takes one in each hand.)

HAROLD: I'm sorry it had to end this way – but I'll come and see you – when the pressure's off. Cheerio, then.

ALBERT: Cheerio.

(Harold strains at the shafts. Nothing happens.)

HAROLD: Is that brake off?

ALBERT: Yeah.

HAROLD: Well, I'll be off, then. Right. Cheerio.

ALBERT: Cheerio.

HAROLD: No hard feelings?

ALBERT: No.

HAROLD: It's the only way. If you don't look out for yourself, you don't deserve to get on. I was in a rut, you see. If I don't go now I'll never go.

ALBERT: Cheerio, then.

HAROLD: Cheerio, then.

(Harold strains harder and harder. The cart doesn't budge.)

ALBERT: I'll go and open the gates, shall I?

(Harold strains and strains, gradually getting weaker. He relaxes, then has another go, panting with the effort. Gradually he starts whimpering.)

HAROLD: Move — move, you rotten stinking cart . . . move . . . I got to go . . . I got to get away . . . move . . . move . . .

(The cart doesn't move. Harold gradually breaks down. Finally he is slumped over one of the shafts sobbing. Albert comes up to him, stands looking at him for a moment, then puts an arm round him and helps him up.)

ALBERT: I'll go and put the kettle on and make a cup of tea, shall I? I'll get the old sausages going — you like sausages, don't you. *(Leading Harold towards the room.)* It's a bit late to start going anywhere now, anyway, isn't it — I mean, it's dark, you'd have to put lights on.

HAROLD: I'm still going . . . I'm not staying . . .

ALBERT: 'Course you're not . . . you can go some other day . . . on a Sunday when the traffic's not so heavy. We'll unload the cart in the morning, don't you worry about that.

(They walk across the yard to the door.)

HAROLD: I'm going . . . I'm not staying here . . . I'm going to take that offer . . .

ALBERT: 'Course you are. They'll keep that offer open for
you – you can go another day. Or you could stay with
your old dad and wait till a better offer comes along – I
mean, look at the way you've saving up stock here . . .
you'll be be a force to be contended with . . . I mean, the
more you have to put down, the better offer you'll get, see
. . . you stay with your old dad . . .
*(They go into the room. Albert comes out again, takes the
barometer from under the tarpaulin, and goes back into the
room, shutting the door after him. The camera tracks back to
take in the cart loaded up in the middle of the yard. Fade
out.)*

DISCOGRAPHY

Not all the material quoted in this book has been issued on gramophone records. Items which have are listed below. All known British issues are listed; many of them have since been deleted. Musicassettes are not included.

'AT LAST THE 1948 SHOW' – 'Bookshop'
Pye NPL 18198

ROWAN ATKINSON – 'Schoolmaster'
Island ILPS 9601

ALAN BENNETT – 'Telegram'
Polydor 582 037; Transatlantic TRA 331 (different versions)

PETER COOK – 'Miner' ('Sitting on a bench')
Capitol ST 11654; Parlophone 45-R 4969, GEP 8940

THE FROST REPORT – 'Class'
Pye NPL 18199, IIPP 201, Golden Hour GH 530

'THE GOON SHOW' – 'Dishonoured – Again'
Parlophone PMC 1108, PMC 7179

TONY HANCOCK – 'The Blood Donor'
Studio recording – Pye-Nixa PLP 1092; Pye NPL 18068; Pye Golden Guinea GGL 0270; Marble Arch MAL 872; Hallmark HMA 228; extracts on Pye NEP 24175; World Record Club-Pye ST 897 Ronco-Charisma RTD 2067

THE MARX BROTHERS – 'A Night at the Opera'
Re-sound RST 7051 (import)

'MONTY PYTHON'S FLYING CIRCUS' – 'Parrot sketch'
BBC Records REB 73; Charisma CLASS 4; Charisma CAS 1134; Arista 4073, AS 0130 (different versions)

Also by Roger Wilmut in Methuen Paperbacks

From Fringe to Flying Circus

Celebrating a Unique Generation of Comedy
1960-1980

'*From Fringe to Flying Circus*', is precisely that, a lovingly written and produced history of the 20 years of stage, radio and TV comedy that began with the four shorthaired satirists of *Beyond the Fringe* in 1960 and which now zooms off into the stratospheric ruderies of *Monty Python*.'
Robert Hewison *The Evening Standard*

'Clever Mr Roger Wilmut has managed to dissect and describe a certain stream of recent humour – the satire of the 1960s and the surreal zaniness of the 1970s – without losing any of the fun of it.'
The Economist

'A very welcome, often very funny book. . . .'
The Paperback and Hardback Buyer

A Methuen Paperback

Monty Python Books in Methuen Paperbacks

MONTY PYTHON'S BIG RED BOOK
THE BRAND NEW MONTY PYTHON
PAPPERBOK
MONTY PYTHON AND THE HOLY GRAIL
(BOOK)
MONTY PYTHON'S LIFE OF BRIAN
MONTY PYTHON'S THE MEANING OF LIFE

Other Silly Books in Methuen Paperbacks

Graham Chapman
A LIAR'S AUTOBIOGRAPHY

Terry Gilliam
ANIMATIONS OF MORTALITY

Robert Hewison
IRREVERENCE, SCURRILITY, PROFANITY,
VILIFICATION AND LICENTIOUS ABUSE:
MONTY PYTHON THE CASE AGAINST

Eric Idle
THE RUTLAND DIRTY WEEKEND BOOK
PASS THE BUTLER

Roger McGough with drawings by Terry Gilliam
SPORTING RELATIONS

Michael Palin and Terry Jones
RIPPING YARNS
MORE RIPPING YARNS

Michael Palin
THE MISSIONARY

For Amnesty International
THE SECRET POLICEMAN'S OTHER BALL

Cartoon Books in Methuen Paperbacks

Bill Tidy

Thelwell

*Other humorous and diverting books
in Methuen Paperbacks*

Kenneth Baker (editor)
I HAVE NO GUN BUT I CAN SPIT

Lisa Birnbach
THE OFFICIAL PREPPY HANDBOOK

Arthur Block
MURPHY'S LAW VOL I
MURPHY'S LAW VOL II
MORE MURPHY'S LAW

Eleanor Bron
LIFE AND OTHER PUNCTURES

Sandra Boynton
CHOCOLATE: THE CONSUMING PASSION

Jilly Cooper
SUPER MEN AND SUPER WOMEN
WORK AND WEDLOCK

Graeme Garden
THE SEVENTH MAN

Frank Muir and Patrick Campbell
CALL MY BLUFF

Frank Muir and Denis Norden
THE 'MY WORD!' STORIES
TAKE MY WORD FOR IT!
OH MY WORD!

Bill Oddie:
BILL ODDIE'S LITTLE BLACK BIRD BOOK

Katharine Whitehorn
WHITEHORN'S SOCIAL SURVIVAL
HOW TO SURVIVE IN HOSPITAL
HOW TO SURVIVE CHILDREN
HOW TO SURVIVE IN THE KITCHEN